SRA
ART
Connections

Level 2

Authors

Rosalind Ragans, Ph.D., Senior Author

Willis "Bing" Davis   Jane Rhoades Hudak, Ph.D.   Bunyan Morris
Tina Farrell   Gloria McCoy   Nan Yoshida

Contributing Author

Jackie Ellett

Education Division
The Music Center of Los Angeles County

Columbus, OH

The McGraw·Hill Companies

Authors

Senior Author
Dr. Rosalind Ragans, Ph.D.
Associate Professor Emerita
Georgia Southern University

Willis "Bing" Davis
Associate Professor Emeritus
Central State University - Ohio
President & Founder of
SHANGO: The Center for the
Study of African American
Art & Culture

Tina Farrell
Assistant Superintendent
Curriculum and Instruction
Clear Creek Independent
School District,
League City, Texas

Jane Rhoades Hudak, Ph.D.
Professor of Art
Georgia Southern University

Gloria McCoy
Former President
Texas Art Education Association
Spring Branch Independent
School District, Texas

Bunyan Morris
Art Teacher
Effingham County School
System, Springfield, Georgia

Nan Yoshida
Art Education Consultant
Retired Art Supervisor
Los Angeles Unified
School District
Los Angeles, California

SRAonline.com

Send all inquiries to:
SRA/McGraw-Hill
8787 Orion Place
Columbus, OH 43240-4027

Printed in the United States of America.

ISBN 0-07-601821-0

1 2 3 4 5 6 7 8 9 RRW 10 09 08 07 06 05 04

Contributors

Contributing Author
Jackie Ellett
Elementary Art Teacher
Duncan Creek Elementary School
Hoschton, Georgia

Artsource® Music, Dance, Theatre Lessons
Mark Slavkin, Vice President for Education
The Music Center of Los Angeles County
Michael Solomon, Managing Director
Music Center Education Division
Melinda Williams, Concept Originator and Project Director
Susan Cambigue-Tracey, Project Coordinator and Writer
Madeleine Dahm, Movement and Dance Connection Writer
Keith Wyffels, Staff Assistance
Maureen Erbe, Logo Design

More about Aesthetics
Richard W. Burrows
Executive Director, Institute for Arts Education
San Diego, California

Safe Use of Art Materials
Mary Ann Boykin
Director, The Art School for Children and Young Adults
University of Houston—Clear Lake
Houston, Texas

Museum Education
Marilyn J. S. Goodman
Director of Education
Solomon R. Guggenheim Museum
New York, New York

Resources for Students with Disabilities
Mandy Yeager
Ph.D. Candidate
The University of North Texas
Denton, Texas

Music Connections
Kathy Mitchell
Music Teacher
Eagan, Minnesota

Student Activities

Cassie Appleby
Glen Oaks Elementary School
McKinney, Texas

Maureen Banks
Kester Magnet School
Van Nuys, California

Christina Barnes
Webb Bridge Middle School
Alpharetta, Georgia

Beth Benning
Willis Jepson Middle School
Vacaville, California

Chad Buice
Craig Elementary School
Snellville, Georgia

Beverly Broughton
Gwinn Oaks Elementary School
Snellville, Georgia

Missy Burgess
Jefferson Elementary School
Jefferson, Georgia

Marcy Cincotta-Smith
Benefield Elementary School
Lawrenceville, Georgia

Joanne Cox
Kittredge Magnet School
Atlanta, Georgia

Carolyn Y. Craine
McCracken County Schools
Mayfield, Kentucky

Jackie Ellett
Duncan Creek Elementary School
Hoschton, Georgia

Tracie Flynn
Home School
Rushville, Indiana

Phyllis Glenn
Malcom Bridge Elementary
Bogart, Georgia

Dallas Gillespie
Dacula Middle School
Dacula, Georgia

Dr. Donald Gruber
Clinton Junior High School
Clinton, Illinois

Karen Heid
Rock Springs Elementary School
Lawrenceville, Georgia

Alisa Hyde
Southwest Elementary
Savannah, Georgia

Kie Johnson
Oconee Primary School
Watkinsville, Georgia

Sallie Keith, NBCT
West Side Magnet School
LaGrange, Georgia

Letha Kelly
Grayson Elementary School
Grayson, Georgia

Diane Kimiera
Amestoy Elementary School
Gardena, California

Desiree LaOrange
Barkley Elementary School
Fort Campbell, Kentucky

Deborah Lackey-Wilson
Roswell North Elementary
Roswell, Georgia

Dawn Laird
Goforth Elementary School
Clear Creek, Texas

Mary Lazzari
Timothy Road Elementary School
Athens, Georgia

Michelle Leonard
Webb Bridge Middle School
Alpharetta, Georgia

Lynn Ludlam
Spring Branch ISD
Houston, Texas

Mark Mitchell
Fort Daniel Elementary School
Dacula, Georgia

Martha Moore
Freeman's Mill Elementary School
Dacula, Georgia

Connie Niedenthal
Rushville Elementary
Rushville, Indiana

Barbara Patisaul
Oconee County Elementary School
Watkinsville, Georgia

Elizabeth Paulos-Krasle
Social Circle Elementary
Social Circle, Georgia

Jane Pinneau
Rocky Branch Elementary School
Watkinsville, Georgia

Marilyn Polin
Cutler Ridge Middle School
Miami, Florida

Michael Ramsey
Graves County Schools
Paducah, Kentucky

Rosemarie Sells
Social Circle Elementary
Social Circle, Georgia

Jean Neelen Siegel
Baldwin School
California

Debra Smith
McIntosh County School System
Darien, Georgia

Patricia Spencer
Harmony Elementary School
Buford, Georgia

Melanie Stokes
Smiley Elementary School
Ludowici, Georgia

Rosanne Stutts
Davidson Fine Arts School
Augusta, Georgia

Fran Sullivan
South Jackson Elementary School
Athens, Georgia

Kathy Valentine
Home School
Burkburnett, Texas

Debi West
Rock Springs Elementary School
Lawrenceville, Georgia

Sherry White
Bauerschlog Elementary School
League City, Texas

Patricia Wiesen
Cutler Ridge Middle School
Miami, Florida

Deayna Woodruff
Loveland Middle School
Loveland, Ohio

Gil Young
Beverly Hills Middle School
Beverly Hills, California

Larry A. Young
Dacula Elementary School
Dacula, Georgia

Table of Contents

What Is Art?

Introduction 12
Subject Matter 16
Elements of Art 22
Principles of Art 23

About Art

Art History and Culture 24
Aesthetic Perception 26
Art Criticism 28
Creative Expression 30
Safety 32

▲ **Jacob Lawrence.**
Street Scene (Boy with Kite).

Unit 1 Line and Shape

An Introduction to Line and Shape 34

Lesson	Activity	Medium	
❶ Line Direction	Paper Sculpture of a Playground	Paper	36
❷ Types of Lines	Dream Tree Line Collage	Paper, Mixed Media	40
❸ Calm Lines	Water Scene	Watercolors	44
❹ Active Lines	Abstract Painting	Tempera	48
❺ Geometric Shapes	Construction Paper Picture	Construction Paper	52
❻ Free-Form Shapes	Shadow Puppet	Paper, Tagboard	56

Wrapping Up Line and Shape 60

Artsource® Lesson
Line and Shape in Theatre 63

◀ **Henry Moore.**
Family Group.

Unit 2 Space and Form

An Introduction to Space and Form 64

Lesson	Activity	Medium	
❶ Geometric Forms	Sculpture	Cardboard Forms	66
❷ Free-Form Forms	Relief Describing the Student	Tagboard, Cardboard, Found Objects	70
❸ Body Forms	Body Form	Clay	74
❹ Animal Forms	Utilitarian Clay Animal Form	Clay	78
❺ People and Space	Paper People	Construction Paper	82
❻ Objects and Space	Still Life	Tempera, Chalk	86

Wrapping Up Space and Form 90

Artsource® Lesson
Space and Form in Theatre 93

▲ **Georgia O´Keeffe.**
The Red Poppy.

Unit 3 Color and Value

An Introduction to Color and Value 94

Lesson	Activity	Medium	
❶ Color and Hue	Painting Hidden Under Rainbow Colors	Tempera	96
❷ Warm Hues	Resist	Tempera, Oil Pastel, Crayon	100
❸ Cool Hues	Landscape	Watercolors, Oil Pastel	104
❹ Value	Value Painting	Tempera	108
❺ Light Values	Landscape	Tempera	112
❻ Dark Values	Feeling Painting	Tempera	116

Wrapping Up Color and Value 120

Artsource® Lesson
Color and Value in Dance 123

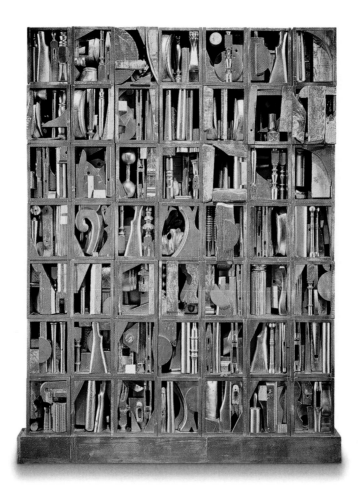

◀ **Louise Nelson.**
Dawn.

Unit 4 Pattern, Rhythm, and Movement

An Introduction to Pattern, Rhythm, and Movement 124

Lesson	Activity	Medium	
❶ Patterns	Sponge Stamp	Tempera, Sponge	126
❷ Patterns in Nature	Glue Drawing	Tempera, Glue, Crayon	130
❸ Rhythm	Still-Life	Tempera, Chalk	134
❹ Rhythm and Form	Storyteller Doll	Clay, Glaze	138
❺ Diagonal Movement	Drawing of Dancing	Computer	142
❻ Curving Movement	Journey Picture	Crayon, Watercolors	146

Wrapping Up Pattern, Rhythm, and Movement 150

Artsource® Lesson
Pattern, Rhythm, and Movement in Storytelling 153

◀ **Chryssa.**
The Gates to Times Square.

Unit 5 Balance, Emphasis, and Texture

An Introduction to Balance, Emphasis, and Texture 154

Lesson	Activity	Medium	
❶ Balance	Paper Jar	Construction Paper	156
❷ Balance in People	Hero Drawing	Crayon, Marker	160
❸ Emphasis	Emphasis Drawing	Marker	164
❹ Emphasis Using Contrast	Night Scene	Oil Pastels	168
❺ Tactile Texture	Stitched Design	Thread, Fabric	172
❻ Visual Texture	Texture Rubbings	Crayon, Marker, Paper	176

Wrapping Up Balance, Emphasis, and Texture 180

Artsource® Lesson
Balance, Emphasis, and Texture in Dance 183

◀ **Diego Velázquez.**
*Las Meninas (The
Maids of Honor).*

Unit 6 Harmony, Variety, and Unity

An Introduction to Harmony, Variety, and Unity 184

Lesson	Activity	Medium	
❶ Harmony of Color	Tile Mural	Tiles, Paint	186
❷ Harmony of Shape and Form	Group of Animals	Computer	190
❸ Variety of Color	Swimmy Print	Paint, Posterboard	194
❹ Variety of Shape and Form	Fantasy Bird	Colored Pencils, Watercolors	198
❺ Unity in Sculpture	Stuffed Paper Animal	Paper, Cardboard Tubes	202
❻ Unity in Architecture	Building Design	Computer	206

Wrapping Up Harmony, Variety, and Unity 210

Artsource® Lesson
Harmony, Variety, and Unity in Dance 213

Technique Tips

Drawing 214

Painting 217

Collage 220

Printmaking 223

Sculpture 225

Needlework 230

Activity Tips

Unit 1 232

Unit 2 235

Unit 3 238

Unit 4 241

Unit 5 244

Unit 6 247

Visual Index 250

Glossary 260

Index 267

What Is Art?

Art is . . .

Painting is color applied to a flat surface.

▲ **Edward Hopper.** (American). *Early Sunday Morning.* 1930.

Oil on canvas. $35\frac{3}{16} \times 60\frac{1}{4}$ inches (89.4 × 153 cm.). Whitney Museum of American Art, New York, New York.

Drawing is the process of making art with lines.

▲ **Pablo Picasso.** (Spanish). *Mother and Child.* 1922.

Oil on canvas. 40 × 32 inches (100 × 81 cm.). The Baltimore Museum of Art, Baltimore, Maryland.

Sculpture is art that fills up space.

▲ **Kiawak Ashoona.** (Inuit). *Seal Hunter.*

Serpentine. Home and Away Gallery, Kennebunkport, Maine.

Architecture is the art of designing and constructing buildings.

▲ **Artist Unknown.** (Roman), *Maison Carée.* 1st century B.C.

Nîmes, France.

Printmaking is the process of transferring an original image from one prepared surface to another.

◀ **Maria Sibylla Merian.** (German). *Plate 2 (from "Dissertation in Insect Generations and Metamorphosis in Surinam").* 1719.

Hand-colored engraving on paper. 18 × 13¾ inches (45.72 × 34.93 cm.). National Museum of Women in the Arts, Washington, D.C.

Pottery is an object made from clay.

▲ **Artist Unknown.** (China). *Covered Jar.* 1522–1566.

Porcelain painted with underglaze cobalt blue and overglaze enamels. 18½ inches high, 15¾ inches in diameter. (7 cm. high, 6 cm. in diameter). Asia Society of New York, New York.

Photography is a technique of capturing an image of light on film.

▲ **Ansel Adams.** (American). *Early Sunday Morning, Merced River, Yosemite Valley, CA.* c. 1950, printed c. 1978.

9⅝ × 12⅞ inches (24.45 × 32.70 cm.). Museum of Modern Art, New York, New York.

A mask is a covering for the face to be used in ceremonies and other events.

◀ **Artist Unknown.** (Ivory Coast). *Senufo Face Mask.* Nineteenth to twentieth century.

Wood, horn, fiber, cloth, feather, metal. 14½ inches tall (35.56 cm.). The Metropolitan Museum of Art, New York, New York.

Art is made by people

▶ to communicate ideas.

▶ to express feelings.

▶ to give us well-designed objects.

What Is Art?

Every work of art has three parts.

Subject

The subject is the object you can recognize in the artwork. If a work has no objects, the elements of art are the subject.

Composition

The composition is how the elements and principles are organized in the artwork.

Content

The content is the message or meaning of the artwork. When the work of art is functional, then the function of the work is the meaning.

▶ In which work of art do you think the subject matter is very important?

▶ In which artwork do you think composition is most important?

▶ Which work seems to have the strongest message? Explain.

▶ Which artwork's meaning relates to its function?

Lorenzo Scott. (American). *Ballet Dancers.*

Oil on canvas. 50 × 30 inches (127 × 76.2 cm.). Collection of Ann and Ted Oliver.

◀ **Joseph Stella.** (American). *The Voice of the City of New York Interpreted/ The Great White Way Leaving the Subway (White Way I).* c. 1920–1922.

Oil and tempera on canvas. $88\frac{1}{2}$ × 54 inches (224.79 × 137.16 cm.). The Newark Museum, Newark, New Jersey.

▲ **Henry Moore.** (British). *Family Group.* 1948–1949.

Bronze (cast 1950), $59\frac{1}{4}$ × $46\frac{1}{2}$ × $29\frac{7}{8}$ inches (150.5 × 118.1 × 75.88 cm.). Museum of Modern Art, New York, New York.

▲ **Caleb Gardner.** (American). *Easy Chair.* 1758.

Walnut, maple, and hand stitched upholstery. $46\frac{3}{8}$ × $32\frac{3}{8}$ × $25\frac{7}{8}$ inches (117.8 × 82.2 × 65.7 cm.). The Metropolitan Museum of Art, New York, New York.

What Is Art?

Subject Matter

Artists make art about many subjects. *Subject matter* is the content of an artist's work. For example, the subject of a painting can be a vase of flowers or a self-portrait. This subject matter is easy to see. The subject matter is harder to understand when the artwork stands for something beyond itself. Look at the artwork on these pages. Notice the different kinds of subject matter.

Still Life

▲ **Paul Cézanne.** (French). *Still Life with Apples. 1895–1898.*

Oil on canvas. 27 × 36½ inches (68.58 × 92.71 cm.). The Museum of Modern Art, New York, New York.

Landscape

▲ **Claude Monet.** (French). *Japanese Bridge over a Pool of Water Lilies.* 1899.

Oil on canvas. $36\frac{1}{2} \times 29$ inches (93 $\times$ 74 cm.). The Metropolitan Museum of Art, New York, New York.

What Is Art?

Genre

▲ **Jacob Lawrence.** (American). *Street Scene (Boy with Kite).* 1962.
Egg tempera on hardboard. $23\frac{7}{8} \times 30$ inches (60.64 × 76.2 cm.). Conservation Center of the Institute of Fine Arts, New York, New York.

Nonobjective

▲ **Joseph Stella.** (American). *The Voice of the City of New York Interpreted/The Great White Way Leaving the Subway (White Way I).* c. 1920–22.

Oil and tempera on canvas. $88\frac{1}{2} \times 54$ inches (224.79 × 137.16 cm.). The Newark Museum, Newark, New Jersey.

What Is Art?

Portrait

▲ **Diego Rivera.** (Mexican). *Kneeling Child on Yellow Background.* 1927.

Oil on canvas. 25½ × 21 inches (65 × 53 cm.). San Francisco Museum of Modern Art, San Francisco, California.

A Story Shown as Symbols

▲ **Artist Unknown.** (English). *The Five Senses: Hearing. (Detail.)* c. 1650–1675.

White satin embroidered in petit point and enriched with seed pearls and coral. Metropolitan Museum of Art, New York.

Elements of Art

Art is a language. The words of the language are the elements of art.

Line

Shape

Form

Space

Color

Value

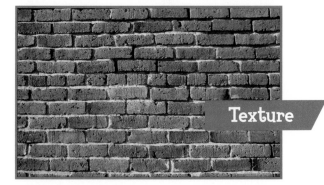

Texture

Principles of Art

Artists organize these words using the principles of art.

Pattern

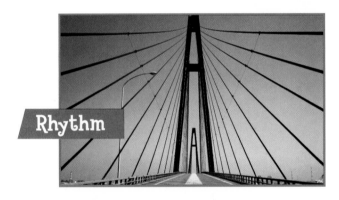

Rhythm

Balance

Emphasis

Harmony

Variety

Unity

About Art

▲ **Horace Pippin.** (American). *Victorian Parlor II.*

1945. Oil on canvas. $25\frac{1}{4} \times 30$ inches (64.1 × 76.2 cm.). The Metropolitan Museum of Art, New York.

Art History and Culture

Look at the artwork.

► What people or objects do you see?
► Do they look like people and objects you see around you today? Explain.

Look at the caption.

► When was the artwork created?
► What can you learn about the artist?

Learn more.

► Do some research to find out more about the artist, the artwork, and the time period.

▲ **Horace Pippin.** (American). *Victorian Parlor II.* 1945.

Oil on canvas. 25$\frac{1}{4}$ × 30 inches (64.1 × 76.2 cm.). The Metropolitan Museum of Art, New York.

Aesthetic Perception

Look

▶ Look at the work of art. What sounds and smells are in this work of art?

▶ What happened just before and just after in this work of art?

Look Inside

▶ Describe the rest of this house. What is in each room?

▶ Tell or write a story about this work of art with a beginning, a middle, and an end.

▶ How would it feel to sit in one of those chairs?

Look Outside

▶ How is this like or different from your own life?

▶ What does the artist want you to know or think about in this work of art?

▶ What will you remember about this work?

About Art

▲ **Horace Pippin.** (American). *Victorian Parlor II.* 1945.

Oil on canvas. $25\frac{1}{4} \times 30$ inches (64.1 × 76.2 cm.). The Metropolitan Museum of Art, New York.

Art Criticism

Describe

▶ List everything you see in this painting.

Analyze

▶ How has the artist used line, shape, color, value, space, and texture?

▶ How has the artist used rhythm, balance, and variety to organize this painting?

Interpret

▶ What is the artist telling you about the people who live in this room?

Decide

▶ Have you ever seen another artwork like this?

▶ Is it successful because it is realistic?

▶ Is it successful because it is well-organized?

▶ Is it successful because you have strong feelings when you study it?

About Art

▲ **Horace Pippin.** (American). *Victorian Parlor II.* 1945.

Oil on canvas. $25\frac{1}{4} \times 30$ inches (64.1 × 76.2 cm.). The Metropolitan Museum of Art, New York.

How does an artist create art? You can follow the same steps to create your own art.

1. Get an idea.
▶ Inspiration comes from many places. Look around you.

2. Plan your work.
▶ Decide what media you want to use. What materials will you need?

3. Make a sketch.
▶ Think about how you want your artwork to look. Sketch several ideas. Then choose the best idea.

4. Use the media.
▶ Make an artwork based on your best idea. You can practice using the materials first.

5. Share your final work.

Safety

▶ Use art materials only on your artwork.

▶ Keep art materials out of your mouth, eyes and ears.

▶ Use scissors carefully. Keep your fingers away from the blades.

▶ Wash your hands after using the art materials.

▶ Wear an art shirt or smock to protect your clothes.

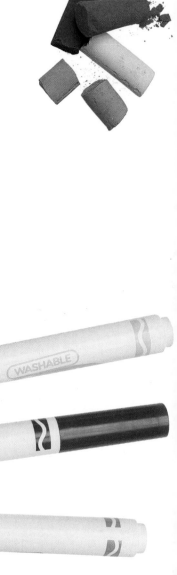

▶ Use only art materials with a "nontoxic" label.

▶ Keep fingers clear when using a stapler.

▶ Be careful not to breathe chalk or clay dust.

▶ Return art materials to their proper storage place.

▶ Always follow your teacher's directions when using art materials.

Line and Shape

▲ **Jacob Lawrence.** (American).
Street Scene (Boy with Kite). 1962.

Egg tempera on hardboard. $23 \frac{7}{8} \times 30$ inches
(60.64 × 76.2 cm). Conservation Center of the
Institute of Fine Arts, New York, New York.

Artists use different kinds of lines to make people, objects, and places.

The lines and shapes make the painting more interesting.

By using different types of lines and shapes, artists can make many objects.

▶ Where do you see straight lines in this painting?

▶ Which objects in the painting are made using curved lines?

▶ Which objects in the painting are made using geometric shapes such as triangles or rectangles?

In This Unit you will learn how artists use lines and shapes to show ideas and feelings. You also will practice using lines and shapes to show your ideas and feelings. Here are the topics you will study:

▶ Line Direction
▶ Line Styles
▶ Calm Lines
▶ Active Lines
▶ Geometric Shapes
▶ Free-Form Shapes

Jacob Lawrence
(1917–2000)

Jacob Lawrence was born in New Jersey. His parents separated when he was seven years old. In 1930 Lawrence's mother brought the children to Harlem in New York City. Lawrence studied arts and crafts there in an after-school program. He painted pictures of his neighborhood and what he saw around him. Lawrence was a pioneer African American artist who also painted pictures about African American history.

Line Direction

Look at the **lines** that are used in these two pieces of art. Trace the outlines of the doors, windows, and shapes on the sculpture with your finger. Trace the lines you see in the painting. Artists use different names to describe lines and the way they move. How many kinds of lines do you see?

◀ **Heron Martínez Mendoza.** (Mexican). *Church.* c. 1960.

Painted earthenware. 24 inches high (60.96 cm.). Museum of International Folk Art, Santa Fe, New Mexico.

 Art History and Culture

These works of art are buildings. How did the artists feel about the buildings? Were they important to them?

Study the **sculpture** and the **painting** to find examples of line direction.

▶ Where in the sculpture and painting do you see diagonal lines?

▶ Where in the sculpture and painting do you see vertical and horizontal lines?

▶ Do you see any other lines in the art?

◀ **Joseph Stella.** (American). *The Voice of the City of New York Interpreted/The Great White Way Leaving the Subway (White Way I).* c. 1920–22.

Oil and tempera on canvas. 88 $\frac{1}{2}$ × 54 inches (224.79 × 137.16 cm.). The Newark Museum, Newark, New Jersey.

Aesthetic Perception

Seeing Like an Artist Look around your classroom and find objects that show lines. In what direction are the lines moving?

Vertical

Horizontal

Diagonal

Zigzag

Curved

Using Line Direction

A line is named for the direction in which it moves. To figure out which direction a line is moving, imagine drawing the line. Which way do you move your pencil to make the line?

Vertical lines move up and down.

Horizontal lines move side to side.

Diagonal lines move from one corner to the opposite corner.

Zigzag lines are made of **angles.**

Curved lines are made of **arcs** instead of straight lines.

Using lines that move in different directions makes artwork more interesting.

Practice

Walk around the room in a line direction.

1. Get into groups and form a line.

2. Walk around the room in the line direction your teacher gives you.

3. Look at how each line moves. Can you see the different line directions?

◄ Anzlee Brock.
Age 7.

Think about how this student used line direction when designing her playground.

Creative Expression

What kind of buildings or structures would you put on a playground? Make a playground from paper using many lines.

1. Think of a playground you would like to create.

2. Twist, curl, and fold strips of paper to make different line directions.

3. Fold the ends of the strips for tabs and glue them onto the base paper to make your playground.

Art Criticism

Describe What equipment is on your playground?

Analyze Which line directions did you use?

Interpret How would your playground look if you used a different line direction?

Decide Could builders construct your playground?

2 Types of Lines

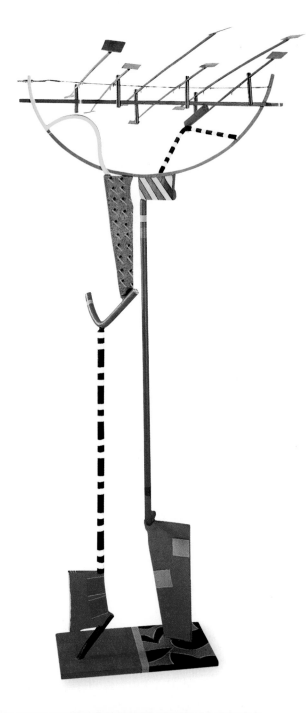

Look at these two pieces of art. *Alanda's Dream Tree* is a sculpture. *Blueberry Eyes* is an oil painting. Both of these works use different line styles. Where do you see a thick line? Where do you see a broken line?

◄ **John T. Scott.** (American).
Alanda's Dream Tree. 1985.

Painted steel, brass, and stainless steel cable. 76 $\frac{1}{2}$ × 36 × 78 inches (194.31 × 91.44 × 198.12 cm.). New Orleans Museum of Art, New Orleans, Louisiana.

 Art History and Culture

Why do you think one artist used a sculpture and the other used a painting to show lines?

Study the works of art to find different line styles.

▶ Do all the lines in the works of art look the same?

▶ What makes some lines look different from others?

▶ How do the different line styles make certain lines stand out?

◀ **Franz Kline.** (American). *Blueberry Eyes.* 1959–1960.

Oil on paperboard. 40 $\frac{1}{8}$ × 29 $\frac{3}{4}$ inches (101.7 × 75.5 cm.). Smithsonian American Art Museum, Washington, D.C.

Aesthetic Perception

Design Awareness Look around the classroom and find an object with lots of lines in it. Can you name the line styles and directions you see?

Using Types of Lines

Lines can be **thick** or **thin, smooth,** or **rough, solid,** or **broken.** The way a line looks is its **style.** Using different line styles can make a work of art more interesting. Different line styles can also describe different moods. Can a line have more than one style?

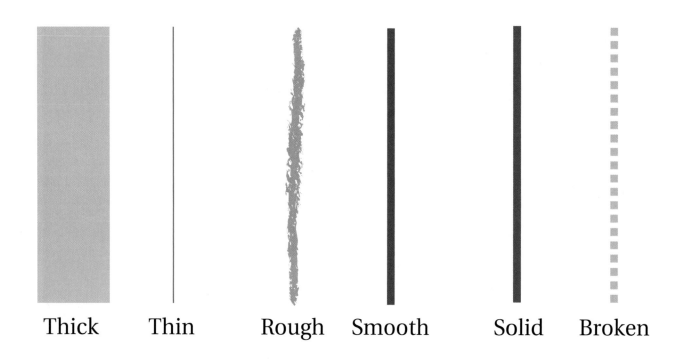

| Thick | Thin | Rough | Smooth | Solid | Broken |

Practice

Create different types of lines.

1. Think of the different types of lines.

2. Look around the classroom for different types of lines.

3. Practice drawing different types of lines on your paper.

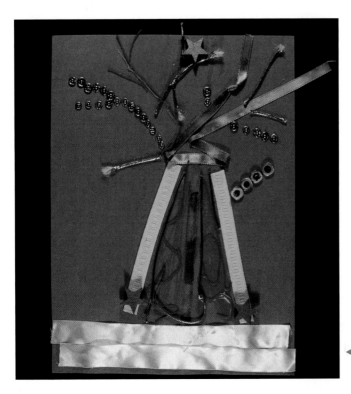

◄ **James Ellis.**
Age 7.

Think about how this student used different types of lines in his dream tree.

 **Creative Expression**

How would you make a dream tree using your imagination? Make a line collage.

1. Draw the lines for your tree with a pencil. Fill the page.

2. Glue line collage materials over the lines.

3. Add objects you like to the branches of the tree. Name your piece.

 **Art Criticism**

Describe What did you put in your dream tree?

Analyze Which kinds of lines did you use the most?

Interpret How would your collage look if you had used only one color?

Decide How else could you arrange your lines?

Calm Lines

◀ **Richard Diebenkorn.**
(American). *Ocean Park
#105.* 1978.

Oil and charcoal on canvas. 99 $\frac{7}{8}$ ×
93 inches (253.7 × 236.2 cm.).
Modern Art Museum of Fort Worth,
Fort Worth, Texas.

Look at these two paintings. Artists use different
kinds of lines in their art to show different
feelings. These artists used horizontal and vertical
lines to create a calm feeling.

 Art History and Culture

Which painting reminds you more of water? Why?

▲ **Claude Monet.** (French).
Palazzo da Mula, Venice.
1908.

Oil on canvas. 24 $\frac{1}{2}$ × 31 $\frac{7}{8}$ inches
(62 × 81.1 cm.). National Gallery of Art,
Washington, D.C.

Study the two works of art to see how the artists used lines to create feelings.

▶ What colors are used in the two paintings?

▶ Where are there horizontal lines in the paintings? Where are there vertical lines?

▶ How do you think the use of horizontal and vertical lines affects the mood of each painting?

Aesthetic Perception

Design Awareness Look at the objects in your classroom. What objects have vertical lines? What objects have horizontal lines?

Using Calm Lines

Artists use different kinds of lines in their art to show different feelings. Horizontal and vertical lines are **calm lines** and give art a calm and quiet look. Can you find the horizontal and vertical lines in the picture below?

Horizontal

Vertical

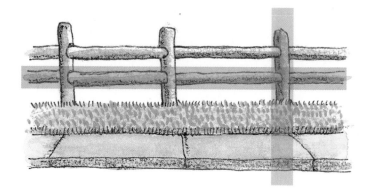

Practice

Try drawing a water object and highlighting the calm lines.

1. Think about something you would find by the water.

2. Try drawing that object using only horizontal and vertical lines.

3. Add color or other line directions for details. Highlight the calm lines in your drawing.

◄ **Zach Rearden.**
Age 7.

Think about how this student used calm
lines in his water scene.

 **Creative Expression**

Make a peaceful water scene using
horizontal and vertical lines.

1. Think of a calm water scene. What
   would you see there?

2. Paint your scene. Fill the paper
   using vertical and horizontal
   brush strokes.

3. Use markers to add details to your
   painting after it is dry.

 **Art Criticism**

Describe What kind of
scene did you paint?

Analyze Which vertical
and horizontal lines stand
out the most?

Interpret How would
your design be different if
you had added other kinds
of lines?

Decide If you wanted to
paint another water scene,
would you use calm lines?

Active Lines

▲ **Wassily Kandinsky.** (Russian).
Composition VI. 1913.
Oil on canvas. 76 ¾ × 118 inches (195 × 300 cm.).
The State Hermitage Museum, St. Petersburg, Russia.

Look at the two works of art. The artists have used many different kinds of active lines to add excitement. Which lines look like they are moving?

 Art History and Culture

Why did these artists make the viewer look closely to see their subjects? Why not paint a realistic picture?

Study both works of art to find examples of active lines.

▶ Which lines give a feeling of movement?

▶ Do any lines seem to be standing still?

▶ How do the active lines make the art feel more exciting?

Aesthetic Perception

Seeing Like an Artist Think of the kinds of lines you could use to describe a ringing telephone.

Using Active Lines

Artists use **active lines** to create motion in a picture and give it a feeling of excitement. They also use active lines when they want the viewer to feel like the art is animated. Diagonal, zigzag, and curved lines are examples of active lines.

Diagonal

Zigzag

Curved

Walk along an active line.

1. Take the piece of yarn your teacher gives you. Remember what color yarn is yours.

2. Lay your yarn on the ground so it forms an active line.

3. Walk back and forth, following the path of your yarn. Look at the paths your classmates are making.

◀ **Kendall Whittlesey.** Age 7.

Think about what kind of event this student could be describing in her abstract painting.

 **Creative Expression**

Can you create an abstract painting of an exciting event using active lines?

1. Think about which lines could describe an exciting event.

2. Draw different active lines with black paint to show the activity in your event.

3. Choose some bright colors and paint the spaces between the black lines.

 **Art Criticism**

Describe Where are the active lines in your picture? Explain your scene.

Analyze Which active lines did you use more than others?

Interpret How would you paint a different event? Would you use different lines?

Decide Could you have painted your event with calm lines?

Geometric Shapes

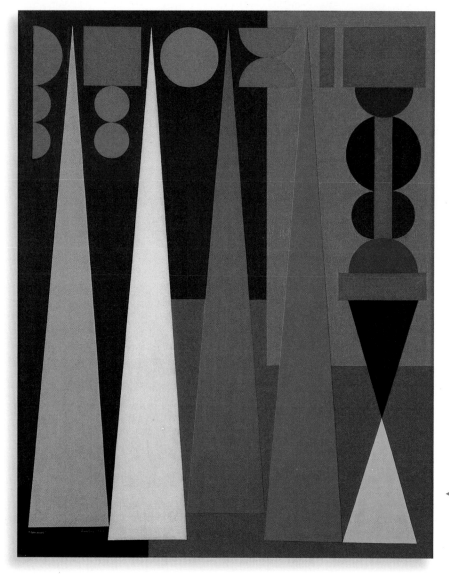

Look at the artwork on these pages. These paintings are made of many shapes. Artists often use **geometric shapes** in their artwork. Can you name all the shapes you see?

◀ **Auguste Herbin.** (French). *Amour.* 1948.
· ·
Oil on canvas. Musée Matisse, Le Cateau-Cambresis, France.

 Art History and Culture

Why do you think these artists used so many geometric shapes in their paintings?

Study both works to find geometric shapes.

▶ What shapes do you see in each work? What colors are they?

▶ Where are the smallest shapes? Where are the largest shapes?

▶ How does the color of some shapes help them stand out?

▲ **Edward Hopper.** (American). *Early Sunday Morning.* 1930.

Oil on canvas. 35 $\frac{3}{16}$ × 60 $\frac{1}{4}$ inches (89.4 × 153 cm.). Whitney Museum of American Art, New York, New York.

Aesthetic Perception

Design Awareness Look outside at a car or truck. Name the geometric shapes that make up the car or truck.

Using Geometric Shapes

Many objects in paintings are made of shapes. These shapes are often geometric shapes. Geometric shapes can be made using special math rules. Not all shapes are geometric, but many common shapes are. Most geometric shapes have names. **Triangles, squares, circles,** and **rectangles** are all geometric shapes.

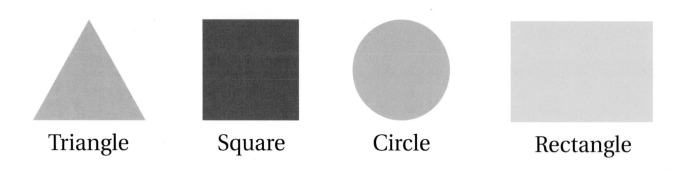

Triangle   Square   Circle   Rectangle

Practice

Make a geometric shape with your classmates.

1. Get into groups. Your teacher will assign your group a shape.

2. Lie on the floor and make that shape.

3. Can you name the shapes other groups made? Can you find something in your room that is your shape?

Think about how this student used geometric shapes in her picture.

Creative Expression

Create a picture using a variety of geometric shapes.

1. Think of a picture you would like to make.
2. Cut out geometric shapes using the colored construction paper.
3. Glue them onto the white paper to create your picture.

Art Criticism

Describe Explain the subject of your picture.

Analyze How did you use geometric shapes to make other shapes?

Interpret What would your picture look like if you had used other shapes?

Decide Do you like the way things look when they are made of only geometric shapes?

Free-Form Shapes

Look at both works of art on these pages. Artists often use **free-form shapes** in works of art. Both of these pieces of art are shadow puppets and were made using free-form shapes.

◀ **Artist Unknown.** (Indonesia). *Indonesian Shadow Puppet.* c. 1950.

Cut, painted leather. 31½ inches high (80.01 cm.). Private Collection.

 Art History and Culture

Why do you think the artists decorated the puppets when audiences see only the puppets' shadows?

Study both works of art to find examples of free-form shapes.

▶ What shapes do you see in both works?

▶ Do you see any geometric shapes?

▶ Can you think of any names to describe the free-form shapes that you see?

◀ **Artist Unknown.** (Thailand). *Thai Shadow Puppet.* c. 1965.

Cut and painted leather. 25 inches tall (63.5 cm.). The Yoshida Collection.

 **Aesthetic Perception**

Seeing Like an Artist Look at free-form shadows in the classroom. Can you identify objects by looking at only the shadows?

Using Free-Form Shapes

Not all shapes in works of art are geometric shapes. Some shapes are free-form shapes. Free-form shapes are **irregular,** and they look different every time they are drawn. Free-form shapes do not have specific names. Some examples of free-form shapes are **splashes, blobs,** and **sails.**

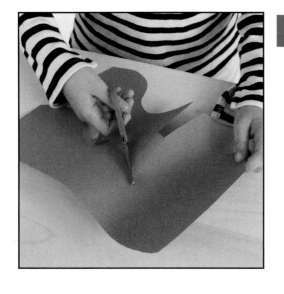

Practice

Create a free-form shape for a shadow puppet.

1. Draw and cut out a free-form shape.
2. Attach it to a stick using a hole punch and a brad.
3. Use your shape to cast a shadow. What does the shadow look like?

Think about where the free-form shapes are in this student's shadow puppet.

◄ **Mandeep Kaur.** Age 7.

 Creative Expression

What kind of shapes could you use to make people? Make a person shadow puppet using body parts.

1. Think of a puppet you would like to create.

2. Draw it and cut out the parts. Add any details to the parts that you wish.

3. Attach moving parts. Tape the puppet to a stick. Add a costume to the puppet using fabric and ribbon.

4. Hold the puppet in front of a light to make a shadow.

 **Art Criticism**

Describe What kind of puppet did you make?

Analyze Which shapes are free-form? Which shapes are geometric?

Interpret How would your design be different if you used only geometric shapes?

Decide If you make another puppet, what will you do differently?

Line and Shape

◀ **William H. Johnson.** (American). *Jitterbugs (II).* c. 1941.

Tempera, pen, and ink with pencil on paper. 17 $\frac{15}{16}$ × 12 $\frac{3}{16}$ inches (40.48 × 30.96 cm.). Smithsonian American Art Museum, Washington, D.C.

Art Criticism Critical Thinking

Describe **What do you see?**

▶ How many people do you see? What are they doing? Describe the room.

Analyze **How is this work organized?**

▶ Where do you see vertical lines? Can you find a horizontal line? Where?

▶ Where do you see diagonal lines? Do you see any curved lines? Where?

▶ Where do you see thick lines? Where do you see rough lines?

▶ Where do you see geometric shapes? Where do you see free-form shapes?

Interpret **What is the artist trying to say?**

▶ Do the lines in this picture make it active or calm?

▶ Is this a happy or sad picture?

▶ What kind of music do you think the people are dancing to?

▶ If you were in this room, what sounds, other than music, would you hear?

Decide **What do you think about the work?**

▶ Is this painting successful because it is realistic, because it is well organized, or because it has a strong message?

Show What You Know

Choose the best answers and write them on a separate sheet of paper.

1 Diagonal, zigzag, and curved lines are all _____.
   A. calm lines
   B. rough lines
   C. active lines

2 _____ can be made using special math rules.
   A. Free-form shapes
   B. Geometric shapes
   C. Active lines

3 _____ and _____ lines are calm lines.
   A. Horizontal, vertical
   B. Curved, smooth
   C. Zigzag, diagonal

4 Two examples of line styles are _____ and _____ .
   A. curved, zigzag
   B. horizontal, vertical
   C. thick, broken

VISIT A MUSEUM
The Smithsonian American Art Museum

The Smithsonian American Art Museum is the largest collection of American art in the world. It is the first national art collection and was started in 1829.

The museum is in the Old Patent Office Building in Washington, D.C. The building was once used as a hospital for soldiers during the Civil War. In 1957 Congress almost tore down the Old Patent Office Building. Instead, they gave the building to the Smithsonian.

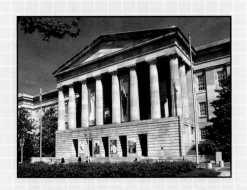

Line and Shape in Theatre

By wearing masks, Robert Faust can become many characters. In many cultures, masks are worn at festivals and celebrations. Masks help a person to pretend to be someone or something else. The lines and shapes used on a mask tell the viewer about the emotions.

What to Do Use lines and shapes to create masks that show two feelings.

1. Discuss opposite feelings such as happy and sad.

2. Create two masks, one for each opposite feeling. Sketch each face on a paper plate. Decorate your masks with shapes and lines. Fasten the two masks to each other so both faces are showing.

3. Cut a slit in the end of a cardboard tube. Put the masks in the slit. Use the tube as a handle.

4. Invent movements to express the feelings on each mask. Perform your expression of opposite feelings for the class.

▲ Robert Faust. "The Mask Messenger"

 **Art Criticism**

Describe Describe your two-sided mask.

Analyze Explain how you used lines and shapes when creating your masks.

Interpret What opposite feelings did you create with your masks and your body?

Decide How well did you express two different emotions in both your mask and movements?

Space and Form

◄ **Henry Moore.** (British).
Family Group. 1948–1949.
....
Bronze (cast 1950). 59 $\frac{1}{4}$ × 46 $\frac{1}{2}$ × 29 $\frac{7}{8}$
inches (150.5 × 118.1 × 75.88 cm.).
Museum of Modern Art, New York,
New York.

Artists use forms to add dimension to their artwork.

Forms are objects that have height, width, and depth. Henry Moore's *Family Group* is a form because it is a statue and has depth.

Forms are like shapes, but forms are three-dimensional. Every shape can be paired with a form.

▶ Why is *Family Group* a form?

▶ Do the forms in *Family Group* match geometric or free-form shapes?

Space is the area around shapes and forms. By using space, artists can make some objects seem closer than others.

▶ Who is closer to you, the mother or the child?

In This Unit you will learn about and make forms. You will also learn how to use space to create depth on a flat surface. Here are the topics you will study:

▶ Geometric Forms

▶ Free-Form Forms

▶ Body Forms

▶ Animal Forms

▶ People and Space

▶ Objects and Space

Henry Moore
(1898–1986)

Henry Moore was born in England. When he was young, he decided he wanted to be a sculptor, but he became a teacher instead. Moore was a soldier in World War I. When he returned home, he went to art school. Moore made abstract figures based on the natural qualities of the materials he used. He was inspired by things he saw during his walks in the fields.

Geometric Forms

Look at both **sculptures.** These sculptures were made using **geometric forms.** Using **forms** adds **depth** and **dimension** to artwork. If you saw these sculptures in a museum, you would be able to walk around them and see every side of the art.

◄ **David Smith.** (American). *Cubi XVIII.* 1964.
Polished stainless steel. 115 ¾ × 60 × 21 ¾ inches (294 × 152.4 × 55.2 cm.). Museum of Fine Arts Boston, Boston, Massachusetts.

 Art History and Culture

Look at the materials these artists used. Why do you think these materials work well for geometric forms?

Study the two sculptures. Think about how the artists used geometric forms.

▶ What forms do you see in the two sculptures? What shapes would they be paired with?

▶ What do you think you would see if you looked at the backs of the sculptures?

◀ **Jesús Moroles.** (American). *Georgia Stele.* 1999.

Georgia gray granite. 82 × 12 $\frac{1}{4}$ × 8 inches (208.28 × 31.12 × 20.32 cm.). Smithsonian American Art Museum, Washington, D.C.

Aesthetic Perception

Design Awareness Can you think of a time you have seen a geometric form? Can you find a geometric form in your classroom now?

circle

cylinder

Using Geometric Forms

square

cube

Geometric forms are similar to geometric shapes. Geometric forms are different because they are **three-dimensional.** A dimension is a measurement. Shapes are **two-dimensional** because they have **height** and **width.** Forms have height, width, and depth. Look at these geometric shapes and forms. Can you see how they match? Can you see how they are different?

triangle

pyramid

Create a geometric form with your classmates.

1. Stand in a horizontal line with one other classmate.

2. Have one classmate line up behind each of you.

3. What geometric form have you made? How many people high is your form? How many people wide is your form? How many people deep is your form?

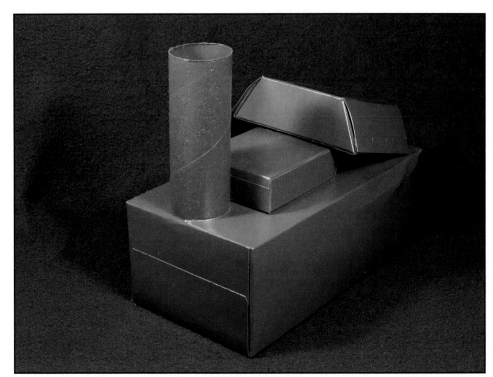

◀ **Matthew Ellett.**
Age 6.

Think about how this student used geometric forms in his sculpture.

 **Creative Expression**

How could you stack geometric forms to create a sculpture? Make a sculpture by stacking and taping geometric forms.

1. Look at your teacher's selection of geometric forms. Think about how you would stack the forms. Plan your design.

2. Select three forms you want to work with. Stack and tape the forms.

 **Art Criticism**

Describe How did you create your sculpture?

Analyze Which geometric forms did you use?

Interpret How would your art be different if you had used shapes instead of forms?

Decide If you made another sculpture to create a series, what would it look like?

Free-Form Forms

◀ **Artist Unknown.** (Iran).
Plate with King Hunting Rams.
Late fifth century A.D. Sasanian
period.

Silver with mercury gilding and niello inlay.
Diameter 8 $\frac{5}{8}$ inches (21.9 cm.). The
Metropolitan Museum of Art, New York,
New York.

Look at the two works of art. Both use free-form forms in their designs. The designs are made using reliefs. A **relief** is a type of sculpture that is made from forms sticking out from a flat background.

 Art History and Culture

Both works of art were made to honor kings. What does this tell you about kings in ancient civilizations?

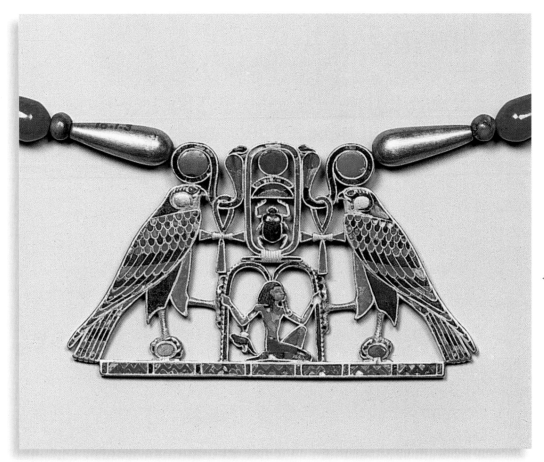

Study the two works of art to look for free-form forms.

▶ What forms are most noticeable?

▶ What shapes do you think match the forms you see?

▶ Do you see any geometric forms?

Aesthetic Perception

Design Awareness Look at the supplies on your desk. Can you find free-form forms in any of the supplies?

Using Free-Form Forms

Free-form forms are also three-dimensional. Like free-form shapes, free-form forms do not have set shapes. Artists use free-form forms to show things like trees and abstract objects in sculptures.

Practice

Can you make a free-form form? Use aluminum foil to practice.

1. Pinch and shape aluminum foil into a free-form form.

2. Does your form look the same as your classmates' forms or is it different?

◀ **Matia Rujiraviriyapinyo.**
Age 8.

Think about how this student showed free-form forms in her relief.

Creative Expression

How would you use a relief to describe yourself? Create a relief using free-form forms.

1. Think about things you like or that describe you. What free-form forms will you use to show these things?

2. Paint a background on tagboard.

3. Draw your forms on cardboard, decorate them, and cut them out.

4. Glue your free-form forms onto the background.

Art Criticism

Describe How does your relief describe you?

Analyze What free-form forms did you use?

Interpret How would your design look if you had used shapes?

Decide Are there times when you think it is better to use forms instead of shapes?

Body Forms

◀ **Roxanne Swentzell.** (Pueblo). *The Emergence of the Clowns.* 1988.

Coiled and scraped clay. Approx. 22 × 50 × 44 inches (55.88 × 127 × 111.76 cm.). Heard Museum, Phoenix, Arizona.

Look at the **statues** on these pages. *The Emergence of the Clowns* was made by layering **coils** of clay and then scraping them so they look smooth. *Seal Hunter* was carved from one piece of stone using **hand tools**. Both artists made **body forms**.

 Art History and Culture

What role do you think clowns and hunters played in the societies these statues were created in?

Study the two statues to learn more about body forms.

▶ What do you think the people in the statues are doing?

▶ How do the artists use forms to make the statues seem alive?

Aesthetic Perception

Seeing Like an Artist Look closely at the people you see every day. Every person has a different body form. Describe some of the forms using art terms.

Using Body Forms

Body forms are three-dimensional versions of body shapes.

Body forms can be shown in many different positions, just like real bodies. Bodies are forms because they have height, width, and depth.

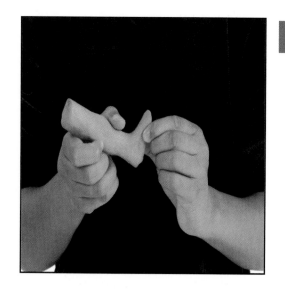

Make a hand or foot out of clay.

1. Use the clay your teacher gives you to make a hand or foot.

2. Pinch apart the clay to make fingers or toes. Think about how hands and feet work.

3. Look around at other students' work. Can you see what they created?

◀ **Sarah Leggett.**
Age 7.

Think about how this student described herself using body forms.

Creative Expression

Can you make a body form to describe your culture?

1. Decide how your body form will represent your culture.

2. Make the parts of your body form from the clay your teacher gives you. Join the pieces together using slip and scoring.

3. Add details to your body form by using a pencil to etch lines and shapes.

Art Criticism

Describe How did you illustrate your culture in your body form?

Analyze Where are the three dimensions in your form?

Interpret What would you title your body form?

Decide What other forms could you make to illustrate your culture?

Animal Forms

◀ **Attributed to John Bell.** (American). *Figure of a Lion.* c. 1850–1860.

· · · · · · · · · · · · · · · · · · ·

Glazed red earthenware. 8 x 8 $\frac{1}{2}$ × 4 $\frac{1}{2}$ inches (20.32 × 21.59 × 11.43 cm.). American Folk Art Museum, New York, New York.

Look at these two animals. The lion was used as a doorstop and is **earthenware.** The leopard is a special type of pitcher and is **brass.** Both of these are **animal forms.**

Art History and Culture

Why do you think the artists chose to use animal forms for these household tools?

Study the two animals and look at their forms.

▶ Do the animals look like they are moving or like they are standing still?

▶ Are the animals realistic?

▶ What do you think these animal forms were used for?

Aesthetic Perception

Seeing Like an Artist Look at your pet or favorite stuffed animal. Can you see the animal form?

Using Animal Forms

Artists use animal forms to show viewers all parts of an animal. Like people, animals have height, width, and depth. When an artist uses an animal form, we can see what the animal looks like from all angles.

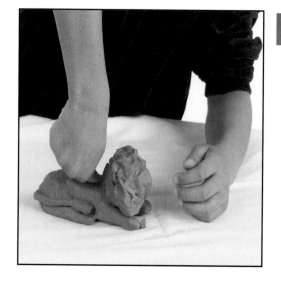

Practice

Can you make a form that can also be used as a bowl? Practice making forms.

1. Think about your favorite animal.

2. Mold your animal form out of clay.

3. Make a depression in your animal form so it can be used as a bowl.

◀ **Jessica Chase.**
Age 8.

Think about how this student created an animal form. How could it be used as a tool?

 **Creative Expression**

How would you make an animal form tool? Construct an animal form using clay.

1. Think about a four-legged animal form you would like to make.

2. Create your animal form. Score your clay and use slip when joining two pieces.

3. Carve details in the clay.

 **Art Criticism**

Describe How did you create your animal form?

Analyze Where is the depth on your animal form?

Interpret How is your animal form different from an animal shape?

Decide How could you use your animal form as a tool?

People and Space

Look at the girls in these paintings. You cannot see the entire girl in the center of *Jungle Tales*. Other bodies **overlap** the girl and hide her. In *Two Sisters,* the younger sister overlaps the older sister. Overlapping creates depth in a painting.

▲ **James J. Shannon.** (American). *Jungle Tales.* 1895.

Oil on canvas. 34 $\frac{1}{2}$ × 44 $\frac{3}{4}$ inches (86.99 × 113.67 cm.). The Metropolitan Museum of Art, New York, New York.

 Art History and Culture

What do these paintings tell you about the role of women in families at this time?

Study the two works of art to find overlapping people.

▶ What are the people doing in these two works of art?

▶ What parts of people are covered up by overlapping?

▶ Which people are farther away from you?

◀ **Auguste Renoir.** (French). *Two Sisters (On the Terrace).* 1881.

Oil on canvas. 40 × 32 inches (100.5 × 81 cm.). The Art Institute of Chicago, Chicago, Illinois.

Aesthetic Perception

Seeing Like an Artist Think about what your family looks like when you sit or stand together. Do any of you overlap?

Using People and Space

Because paintings are two-dimensional, artists can't use forms. To show depth, artists use overlapping.

By hiding part of a person, artists make it seem as if the person is behind something. That makes the viewer think the person is farther away and creates depth. Look at the picture. Which person is closest to you? Which person is farthest away?

Assemble in a group of classmates so that you overlap and create depth.

1. Break up into small groups.

2. Position yourselves so you are all overlapping.

3. Look at your group. Do you see that the person in front is overlapped by no one? Do you see that the person in back is overlapped by several people?

Think about how this student used overlapping to show her family playing.

🎨 Creative Expression

What does a family on a playground look like from far away? Overlap shapes of people playing.

1. Think about the way your body moves when you play.

2. Use construction paper and draw a family playing. Cut out the shapes.

3. Arrange and overlap your family on white paper. Move them around until you like the way they look. Glue the shapes onto the paper.

❗❓ Art Criticism

Describe What is the family in your picture doing?

Analyze Find the places in your design where figures overlap.

Interpret How would your design look different if none of the figures overlapped?

Decide What other kinds of activities could you use to show a family overlapping?

Objects and Space

▲ **Louise Moillon.** (French).
*Still Life with Cherries,
Strawberries, and
Gooseberries.* 1630.
....
Oil on panel. 12 $\frac{5}{8}$ × 19 $\frac{1}{8}$ inches
(30.07 × 48.58 cm.). Norton Simon
Museum, Pasadena, California.

Look at these two paintings. They are still lifes. A **still life** is a painting or drawing of a collection of objects that cannot move. Which objects overlap others in these paintings? Which objects are closest to you?

 Art History and Culture

Why do you think these artists used fruit in their paintings instead of other foods?

▲ **Paul Cézanne.** (French).
Still Life with Apples.
1895–1898.

Oil on canvas. 27 × 36 ½ inches
(68.58 × 92.71 cm.). The
Museum of Modern Art, New York,
New York.

Study the two still lifes to find overlapping objects.

▶ What objects do you see in the two paintings? Point out an object that is overlapped by another.

▶ Which objects are farthest away from you?

Aesthetic Perception

Design Awareness Think about food you see at the grocery store. Do you see overlapping in the displays? Why do stores do this?

Using Objects and Space

Because paintings are two-dimensional, artists can't use forms to show depth. We see depth in still-life paintings and drawings when artists overlap objects.

Hiding part of an object creates depth and makes the viewer think the object is farther away. Look at the picture. Which object is closest to you? Which object is farthest from you?

Practice

Set up a still life on your desk.

1. Pick three or four objects from your teacher's collection.

2. Arrange the objects on your desk so some of them overlap.

3. Sketch the still life you have created for practice. Make sure you pay attention to which parts of the objects are hidden by overlapping.

◀ **Joseph Williams.**
Age 7.

Think about how this student arranged his still life to create depth.

Creative Expression

What kinds of foods would you put in a still life? Arrange and paint a still life using overlapping.

1. Think of some objects and foods you would like to draw. Use all different kinds of forms.

2. Arrange your objects so some overlap.

3. Start by drawing the objects closest to you. Then draw the objects that are farther away.

4. Paint your still life.

Art Criticism

Describe What foods did you use in your still life?

Analyze Where is the overlapping in your still life?

Interpret Which objects were farthest away? Which were closest?

Decide What other healthy foods could you have used in your still life?

Space and Form

▲ **Yoruba People.** (Nigerian). *Headdress for Epa Masquerade.* c. 20th century.

Carved wood and pigment. 50 × 20 × 18 inches (127 × 50.8 × 45.72 cm.). Birmingham Museum of Art, Birmingham, Alabama.

! Art Criticism Critical Thinking

Describe What do you see?

▶ Read the credit line to find out what this object is, what it is made of, and how big it is. Is it taller or shorter than you?

▶ Describe the parts of this object.

Analyze How is this work organized?

▶ Where do you see geometric and free-form forms on this headdress?

▶ Where do you see a body form and an animal form?

Interpret What is the artist trying to say?

▶ What do you think this headdress is used for?

▶ How do you think it would feel to cover your body with long leaves and put this on your head?

▶ How would you move when wearing this?

▶ Write a short poem to say while wearing this headdress.

Decide What do you think about the work?

▶ Is this headdress successful because it is realistic, because it is well organized, or because it has a strong message? Explain.

Show What You Know

Select the best answers to these questions. Write your answers on a separate sheet of paper.

1 Forms have height, width, and _____.
A. space
B. depth
C. lines

2 The difference between shapes and forms is that forms are _____.
A. three-dimensional
B. large
C. smooth

3 Artists use _____ to create depth in a painting.
A. glitter
B. overlapping
C. still lifes

4 A _____ is a painting or drawing of a collection of objects that cannot move.
A. portrait
B. still life
C. relief

CAREERS IN ART
Florist

Have you ever seen flower arrangements in a vase or park? These flowers were arranged by someone who made careful decisions about space and form when putting together the design.

Florists must be able to plan a design based on the forms and colors of the flowers they are using.

Botanical curators design where to place outdoor plant exhibits in botanical gardens based on space so the plants look their best.

▲ Florist

Space and Form in Theatre

Eth-Noh-Tec, an Asian American Company, combines music, movement, and words in their performances. They use dialogue, body poses, comic facial expressions, and hand gestures. This is based on ancient Asian theatre styles from Chinese and Japanese traditions. They perform Asian stories that have a moral at the end.

▲ Eth-Noh-Tec. "Long Haired Girl."

What to Do Create a frozen picture of a scene from a class story.

1. Divide into groups and take a card that describes one even from the story.

2. Work together to create your frozen scene of that event. One person should be the director.

3. Decide which things will overlap to create depth in your scene. Think about what forms you are making.

4. Have each group present their frozen scene to the class in story order.

 **Art Criticism**

Describe How did you create depth in your frozen scene?

Analyze Explain the decisions you made to create your frozen scene.

Interpret How does your frozen scene express the main idea of your scene.

Decide How well did you capture the mood of your scene?

Color and Value

▲ **Georgia O'Keeffe.**
(American). *The Red Poppy.* 1927.
· ·
Oil on canvas. Private collection.

Artists use color and value to add variety to their artwork.

Georgia O'Keeffe used both **color** and **value** when she painted *The Red Poppy*. In art, color is every color in the **spectrum,** or rainbow, as well as black and white. Only the **spectral colors** are called **hues.** Value is how dark or light a color is.

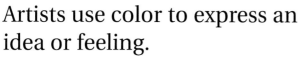

Artists use color to express an idea or feeling.

▶ What color did O'Keeffe use most in this painting?

Artists use value when they want to change how light or dark a color appears.

▶ Where is the red darker and lighter in this painting?

▶ Where are the darkest and lightest areas in the painting?

In This Unit you will learn about and practice mixing colors and creating values. Here are the topics you will study:

▶ Color and Hue
▶ Warm Hues
▶ Cool Hues
▶ Value
▶ Light Values
▶ Dark Values

Georgia O'Keeffe
(1887–1986)

Georgia O'Keeffe decided at a young age to be an artist and studied at the Art Institute of Chicago. She became frustrated with the painting style of her teachers and quit making art. Alfred Steiglitz, a famous photographer and gallery owner, noticed her art and pushed O'Keeffe to paint more. She soon created her own style of painting. O'Keeffe was most famous for painting close-up views of flowers and desert life.

Color and Hue

Look at these two works of art. Artists use color to express themselves. Both artists used spectral colors to make this art.

▲ **Robert Lostutter.**
(American). *Baird Trogon.* 1985.

Watercolor over graphite on paper. 24 $\frac{1}{4}$ × 34 $\frac{5}{8}$ inches (61.5 × 88 cm.). The Art Institute of Chicago, Chicago, Illinois.

 Art History and Culture

Do you think these paintings are modern art? Why?

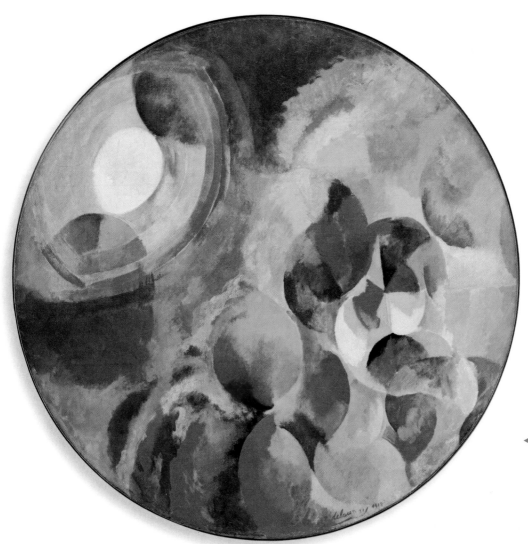

Study both works of art to see how artists use color.

▶ What do you see in these two works of art? Can you find any hidden pictures?

▶ Where do you see colors in these paintings that are not hues?

Aesthetic Perception

Design Awareness Open your crayon or marker box and look at the colors. Where else in the room do you see those colors?

Using Color and Hue

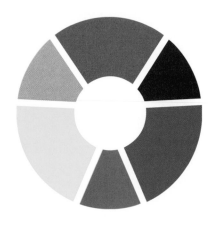

A **color wheel** is a way of organizing the spectral colors, or hues. Red, blue, and yellow are **primary hues.** Orange, green, and violet are **secondary hues.**

Two primary hues mixed together make a secondary hue. No two colors can be mixed to make a primary hue.

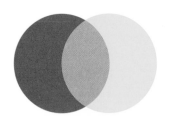  

Practice

Make groups according to the color of your clothing.

1. Look at the colors that your classmates are wearing.

2. Group yourself with other classmates who are wearing the same color shirt.

3. Can you name the colors of the other groups? Are they primary or secondary?

Think about how this student used color and hue.

Creative Expression

Can you hide an object underneath color? Use color to hide a drawing you make.

1. Think of a scene or picture that you would like to draw.

2. Draw the scene on your paper using a black marker. Make your lines very bold.

3. Paint your picture using spectral colors in the correct order.

Art Criticism

Describe Where is the hidden drawing in your picture?

Analyze What colors did you use to hide your drawing?

Interpret How would your picture look different if you had used other colors to hide your drawing?

Decide Which works better for this project, dark or light colors?

Warm Hues

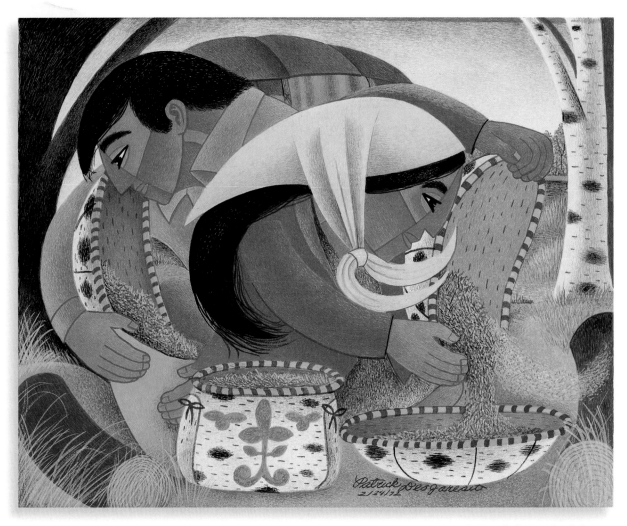

Look at the hues used in these paintings. Both *Gathering Wild Rice* and *Summer's Sunlight* were painted using many yellows, oranges, and reds. These are **warm hues.**

▲ **Patrick DesJarlait.**
(Ojibwe/Chippewa).
Gathering Wild Rice.
1972.

Watercolor on paper. 10 $\frac{9}{10}$ × 15 $\frac{1}{2}$ inches (27.69 × 39.5 cm.).
Heard Museum, Phoenix, Arizona.

 Art History and Culture

In which seasons do you think these scenes take place? Why?

Study the two paintings to find the warm hues.

▶ What items do you see that were painted using warm hues?

▶ How do the warm hues used in these paintings make you feel?

▲ **Beatrice Whitney Van Ness.** (American). *Summer's Sunlight.* c. 1932–1934.

Oil on canvas. 40 × 50 inches (101.6 × 127 cm.). National Museum of Women in the Arts, Washington, D.C.

Aesthetic Perception

Seeing Like an Artist When you look through the window, what things do you see that are warm hues?

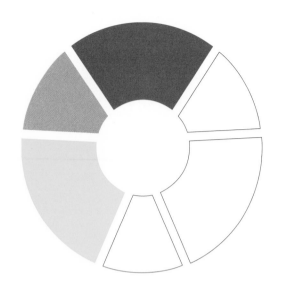

Using Warm Hues

Hues can be divided into two groups. The warm hues are red, orange, and yellow. Warm hues are next to each other on the color wheel. These hues are associated with warm things such as fire or sunshine.

Practice

Use warm hues to write words.

1. Think of words that you associate with the word *warm*.

2. Pick out warm-colored markers or crayons.

3. Make a list of your warm words using warm hues.

◄ **Stefani Brogdan.**
Age 7.

Think about how this student used warm hues for a warm object.

 **Creative Expression**

How can you express a warm object in a piece of art? Make a resist that uses warm hues.

1. Think of an object that reminds you of summer.

2. Draw that item with warm oil pastels.

3. Paint over the drawing using black tempera.

 **Art Criticism**

Describe What warm object did you draw?

Analyze What hues did you use to express your object?

Interpret How do the hues that you used tell a viewer how your object makes you feel?

Decide If you were going to do the same thing with a cold object, what hues would you use?

3 Cool Hues

▲ **Tom Thomson.**
(Canadian). *Spring Ice.* 1916.
....
Oil on canvas. 28 $\frac{1}{3}$ × 40 $\frac{3}{10}$
inches (72 × 102.3 cm.).
National Gallery of Canada,
Ottawa, Ontario, Canada.

Look at the hues used in these works of art. *Spring Ice* and *A View of Mansfield Mountain* were painted using blues, greens, and violets. These hues are known as **cool hues.**

Art History and Culture

Both artists painted many landscapes throughout their careers. What do you think these places meant to them?

Study the two works of art to find cool hues.

▶ What objects in the painting were made using cool hues?

▶ How do the cool hues in the paintings make you feel?

▶ Do you see any warm hues in the paintings?

◀ **John Frederick Kensett.** (American). *A View of Mansfield Mountain.* 1849.

Oil on canvas. 48 × 39 $\frac{5}{8}$ inches (121.92 × 100.7 cm.). Museum of Fine Arts Houston, Houston, Texas.

Aesthetic Perception

Design Awareness Look around your classroom. Can you find three things that are cool hues? Can you think of things in your school that are cool hues?

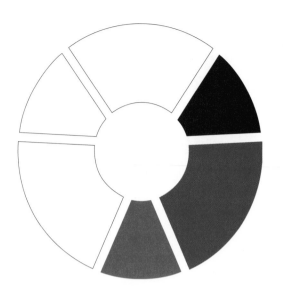

Using Cool Hues

Cool hues are the opposite of warm hues. The cool hues are blue, green, and violet. Cool hues are also next to each other on the color wheel. These hues are associated with cool things such as snow, water, and grass.

Practice

Create an imaginary plant using cool hues.

1. Use your imagination and think of a plant that would be in your perfect backyard.

2. Draw the plant using crayons or markers.

3. Use cool watercolors to paint the plant.

◄ **Xavier Andrews.**
Age 7.

Think about how this student painted his perfect backyard using cool hues.

 **Art Criticism**

Creative Expression

What would your perfect backyard look like? Make a painting of your landscape using cool hues.

1. Think about your perfect backyard. What would it look like? What would be there?

2. Paint the background for your landscape using cool watercolors.

3. Add details to your painting using cool oil pastels or tempera paints.

Describe What did you choose to put in your landscape?

Analyze Which cool hues did you choose?

Interpret How would your landscape be different if you had used only warm hues?

Decide If you added accents of warm hues, what effect would they have on your landscape?

Value

Look at these two **photographs.** Both *The Flatiron* and *Early Sunday Morning, Merced River, Yosemite Valley, CA* were taken using black and white film. Instead of using color, the artists have chosen to express what they see by using value.

◀ **Edward Steichen.** (American).
The Flatiron. 1904, printed 1909.

Gum bichromate over platinum print. 18 $\frac{13}{16}$ × 15 $\frac{1}{8}$ inches (47.78 × 38.42 cm.). The Metropolitan Museum of Art, New York, New York.

 Art History and Culture

These photos show trees in different areas. What can you tell about the neighborhoods from the photographs?

▲ **Ansel Adams.** (American).
*Early Sunday Morning,
Merced River, Yosemite
Valley, CA.* c. 1950,
printed c. 1978.

$9\frac{5}{8} \times 12\frac{7}{8}$ inches (24.45 × 32.70 cm.).
The Museum of Modern Art, New
York, New York.

Study the two photographs to find examples of value.

▶ What is the darkest area in each photograph?

▶ What is the lightest area in each photograph?

▶ What colors do you see in the photographs?

Aesthetic Perception

Design Awareness Look in your crayon or marker box. Can you find three crayons or markers that are different values of the same color?

Using Value

Value describes how light or dark a color is. If the value is darker, then there is more black mixed in with the color. If the value is lighter, then there is more white mixed in with the color.

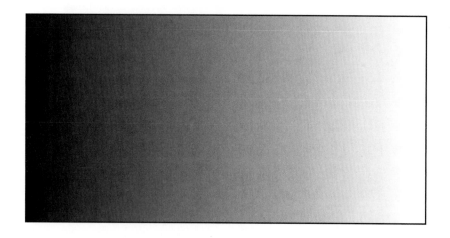

Practice

Make a line with your classmates that shows value.

1. Look at the value on the card your teacher hands you. Is your value dark or light?

2. Hold up your color so people can see it. Compare your value with your classmates' values.

3. Stand in a horizontal line according to your value.

Think about how this student used value in his art.

 **Creative Expression**

Can you paint an object from your neighborhood using dark and light values? Paint a picture using black and white values.

1. Think of an object that you see often in your neighborhood. Paint that object using white paint.

2. Mix black and white paint to create a gray value. Make a gray outline around your object.

3. Mix darker values and continue outlining your object until you make a black line.

Art Criticism

Describe What object did you draw?

Analyze How did you create the darker values? The lighter values?

Interpret How would the painting look if you had started with dark values and worked to light?

Decide What other kinds of drawings would make good designs using values?

Lesson 5 · Light Values

◀ **Jane Wilson.** (American).
Solstice. 1991.

Oil on linen. 60 × 70 inches (152.4
× 177.8 cm.). Fishbach Gallery,
New York, New York.

Look at these two paintings of the American
West. People who lived in the early American
West were surrounded by wide, empty spaces.
Both paintings were made using **light values.**
Could you tell what time of day these paintings
represent by looking at only the colors and
values?

 Art History and Culture

Can you tell how the artists feel about the West by
looking at their paintings?

Study the two paintings to find light values.

► Where are the lightest values in these paintings?

► What kind of mood is created by using the light values?

▲ **Minerva Teichert.**
(American). *Night Raid.*
c. 1935.

Oil on canvas. 45 $\frac{15}{16}$ × 67 $\frac{7}{8}$
inches (116.68 × 172.40 cm.).
Brigham Young University
Museum of Art, Provo, Utah.

Aesthetic Perception

Seeing Like an Artist Look through the window of your classroom. Can you see light values in the hues outside? Where do you see them?

Using Light Values

Value is how light or dark a color is. To create light values, more white is added to a hue. A light value of a hue is called a **tint.**

Practice

Create a drawing of the American West using tints.

1. Think about the history of the American West. Pick an object that reminds you of the American West.

2. Draw the object on your paper.

3. Use tints of colors to color your picture.

◀ **Jessie Little.**
Age 6.

Think about how this student used tints to make a landscape.

 **Creative Expression**

People in the early American West usually lived many miles from their neighbors. What landscape did these people see? Paint the landscape using tints to create a mood picture.

1. Pick three hues. Add small amounts of each hue to white.

2. Think about the scenery that people in the early American West would have seen.

3. Paint your picture using these tints.

Art Criticism

Describe What objects are in your landscape?

Analyze Which hues did you use to make tints?

Interpret How do the light tints create mood in your painting? What mood do you think they create?

Decide If you were going to use dark values in your landscape, where would you put them?

Dark Values

▲ **Adolph Gottlieb.**
(American). *Spectre of the Sea.* 1947.
....
Oil on canvas. 30 × 38 inches
(76.2 × 96.52 cm.). The Montclair
Art Museum, Montclair, New Jersey.

Look at the two paintings on these pages. Both artists used dark values when making their paintings. How do the dark values make you feel?

Art History and Culture

What feelings do you think artists express with dark values?

Study the two works of art to find the dark values.

▶ Where are the darkest values in these paintings?

▶ Why do you think these artists used dark values for these subjects?

▶ What do you imagine is happening in these paintings?

◀ **Harold Town.** (Canadian). *The First Aeroplane.* 1956.
....
Autographic print on woven paper. 25 × 19 inches (63.7 × 48.4 cm.). National Gallery of Canada, Ottawa, Ontario, Canada.

Aesthetic Perception

Design Awareness Look around your room and find three things that are a dark value of red. What are they?

Using Dark Values

Artists create dark values by adding more black to a hue. A dark value is called a **shade.** Shades can be used to create moods in a painting that are dark, gloomy, or mysterious. Can you think of other moods you could create by using shades?

Practice

Use a drawing to express a feeling.

1. Think of different feelings that you want to try to express.

2. Use a crayon or a marker to draw pictures on your paper that represent those feelings to you.

3. Write the name of each feeling under the picture it belongs to.

◀ **Yeji Park.**
Age 7

Think about how this student used dark values to express a feeling.

Creative Expression

How would you represent feelings with pictures? Make a painting using dark values to express feelings.

1. Choose a feeling that you would like to explain using pictures. Pick three colors to use.

2. Mix a small amount of black with each color.

3. Paint your feeling picture using the shades.

Art Criticism

Describe Explain which feeling you showed in your painting.

Analyze Which hues did you use to make the shades?

Interpret How did the shades change the mood of your painting?

Decide If you were to make another painting, what shades would you use?

Color and Value

▲ **Miriam Schapiro.** (American).
Personal Appearance. 1985.
....
Acrylic, fabric, and paper on canvas. 85 × 77
inches (215.9 × 195.58 cm.). Private Collection.

Art Criticism · Critical Thinking

Describe What do you see?

▶ Describe what this person is doing.

▶ Describe the background.

Analyze How is this work organized?

▶ Where do you see primary hues?

▶ Where do you see secondary hues?

▶ Where are the lightest values in the painting? The darkest?

▶ Where do you see warm hues? Cool hues?

Interpret What is the artist trying to say?

▶ Which hues seem more important, the warm or the cool? How do they affect the mood of the painting?

▶ What music would you hear if you were in this painting?

▶ Pose like the woman in the painting. How does that make you feel?

▶ Where do you think this woman is, and who is watching her?

Decide What do you think about the work?

▶ Is this painting successful because it is realistic, well organized, or because it has a strong message? Explain.

Show What You Know

Choose the best answer to each question and write them on a separate sheet of paper.

1 A _____ is created by adding white to a hue.
A. shade
B. primary hue
C. tint

2 Hues are _____.
A. the colors in the spectrum
B. the colors in the spectrum plus black and white
C. shades

3 Another name for dark values is _____.
A. tints
B. shades
C. spectrum

4 Red, yellow, and orange are _____.
A. primary colors
B. cool hues
C. warm hues

VISIT A MUSEUM
The Museum of Modern Art

The Museum of Modern Art in New York City began in 1929 as an educational institution. The creators of the museum wanted a place where people could enjoy art that was being produced at that time. The Museum of Modern Art, or MoMA, has six departments: Architecture and Design, Film and Media, Photography, Painting and Sculpture, Drawings, and Prints and Illustrated Books. MoMA's collection has over 100,000 works of art and is one of the best collections of modern art in the world.

Color and Value in Dance

Lai Haraoba means 'festival of the gods and goddesses. It is an old folk dance from India that is performed during summer. The dance is accompanied by an ancient, one-stringed instrument called a *pena*. The dancers wear colorful costumes and use expressive hand movements called *mudras.*

What to Do Make up a dance with hand movements.

1. Think of ways you can move your hands to express things. For example, how would you express rain? How would you express fish?

2. Pick words and create movements to express them. Practice your movements. What color would your movements be?

3. Choose two movements to teach a partner. Learn your partner's movements.

4. Perform your movements together for the class.

▲ Ranganiketan Manipuri Cultural Arts Troupe. "Lai Haraoba."

 Art Criticism

Describe What two words did you pick and what movements did you use to express them?

Analyze What was the hardest thing about learning your partner's movements?

Interpret How did it feel to combine the four movements and perform them with your partner?

Decide Were you able to create movements that expressed an idea or feeling?

Pattern, Rhythm, and Movement

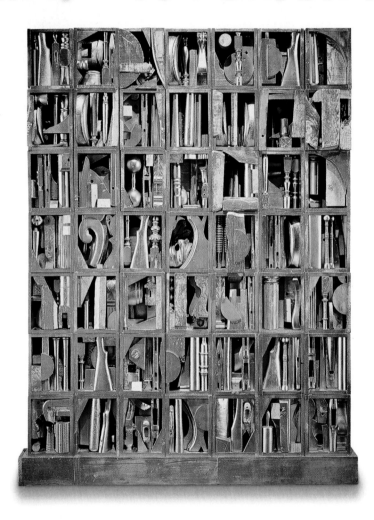

Artists use pattern, rhythm, and movement to make their artwork more interesting and exciting.

Pattern, rhythm, and movement make your eyes move around a work of art.

▲ **Louise Nelson.** (American). *Dawn.* 1962.

Gold painted wood. 94 $\frac{1}{2}$ × 75 $\frac{1}{2}$ × 7 $\frac{3}{4}$ inches (240.03 × 191.77 × 19.7 cm.). The Pace Wildenstein Gallery, New York, New York.

Artists use **pattern** to create a surface design in artwork.

▶ Are there patterns in *Dawn*?

Artists create **rhythm** by repeating shapes or objects in a work of art.

▶ What is repeated in this sculpture?

Artists use **movement** to lead your eyes around a work of art.

▶ What kinds of lines lead your eyes around this sculpture?

▶ Which direction do your eyes move?

In This Unit you will practice techniques to create pattern, rhythm, and movement. Here are the topics you will study:

▶ Pattern
▶ Patterns in Nature
▶ Rhythm
▶ Rhythm and Form
▶ Diagonal Movement
▶ Curving Movement

Louise Nelvelson
(1900–1988)

Louise Nevelson was born in Russia and moved to America when she was five. She was interested in singing and acting, but chose a career in visual arts. Nevelson became famous for her sculptures. She created sculptures by gluing together small pieces of wood that she found and then painting them black, white, or gold. Some of her sculptures are as big as rooms.

Pattern

Look how these works of art use **pattern.** Pattern is made by repeating a **motif.** The *X* on the bag is one motif. Can you see how it is repeated in a pattern?

◄ **Artist Unknown.** (Delaware).
Delaware Shoulder Bag. c. 1860.

Wool and cotton fabric. $8\frac{3}{5} \times 7\frac{4}{5}$ inches (21.9 × 19.7 cm.). Detroit Institute of Arts, Detroit, Michigan.

 Art History and Culture

Can you guess anything about the cultures that made these works of art by studying the art?

◀ **Catherine Fitzgerald.** (American). *Princess Feather and Rising Sun Quilt.* c. 1840–1850.

Cotton pieced and appliquéd. 102 × 93 inches (259.08 × 236.22 cm.). The Newark Museum, Newark, New Jersey.

Study the two works of art. Find examples of patterns and motifs.

▶ What motifs do you see in the shoulder bag?

▶ How are the bag motifs different when they are repeated in the pattern?

▶ What motifs do you see in the quilt?

▶ Are the quilt motifs changed when they are repeated?

Aesthetic Perception

Design Awareness Look around your classroom. Can you find any patterns? Motifs?

Using Pattern

Pattern is a decorative design on the surface of something. Patterns are two-dimensional. The part of the pattern that repeats is the motif.

Motifs do not always look the same in a pattern. A motif can be turned different ways or be different colors. Look at this pattern. Can you see how the motif repeats and changes?

motif

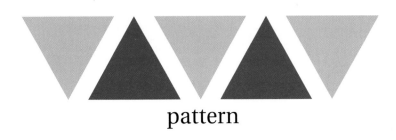

pattern

Practice

Make a pattern with your classmates.

1. Look at the colors and shapes your teacher has given you.

2. Brainstorm with your classmates about a pattern you can make.

3. Line up the shapes so they are in a pattern. What is the motif?

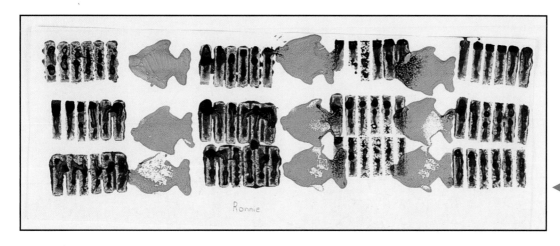

Think about how this student used pattern and motif in his artwork.

🎨 Creative Expression

What kind of patterns could you make that would describe your culture? Design a motif and make a pattern.

1. Think of a motif that describes your culture. Draw the motif and cut it out of a sponge.

2. Dip your sponge into paint. Make prints on the paper using your motif to create a pattern.

3. Fill the paper with your pattern.

Art Criticism

Describe What did you choose for your motif?

Analyze How did you use your motif to make a pattern?

Interpret How does your pattern express your culture?

Decide Did you repeat your motif to make an interesting pattern?

Patterns in Nature

Look at the two pieces of art. Both are realistic illustrations of objects the artists found in nature. Where are patterns in these **prints**?

◀ **Maria Sibylla Merian.** (German). *Plate 2 (from "Dissertation in Insect Generations and Metamorphosis in Surinam").* 1719.

Hand-colored engraving on paper. 18 × 13 ¾ inches (45.72 × 34.93 cm.). National Museum of Women in the Arts, Washington, D.C.

Art History and Culture

How do you think these two artists felt about nature? Why?

Study the two works of art to find examples of patterns in nature.

▶ What patterns do you see in these two pictures?

▶ What are the motifs of the patterns you found?

◀ **John James Audubon.**
(West Indian/American).
Carolina Parakeet. 1832.
....
Aquatint engraving on paper. 33 × 24 inches
(83.82 × 60.96 cm.). The Morris Museum of Art,
Augusta, Georgia.

Aesthetic Perception

Seeing Like an Artist What patterns can you find on plants and animals in your community?

Using Patterns in Nature

Not all patterns are made by a person. Many patterns are in the plants, animals, and other natural objects around us. Look at the photographs below. Can you see the patterns?

Practice

Draw a leaf with a pattern on it.

1. Draw the outline of a leaf.
2. Think of a pattern to put on the leaf.
3. Draw the pattern on the leaf using crayons or markers. What is your motif?

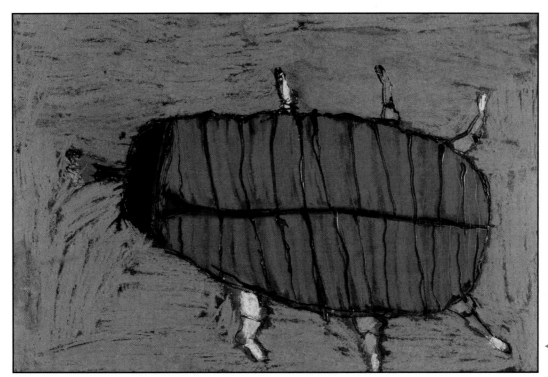

◀ **Mitchell Pettus.**
Age 7.

Think about how this student used pattern on his bug.

 Creative Expression

What kind of patterns have you seen around you? Draw a natural object that has patterns.

1. Think of an animal, plant, or other natural object. Draw a large picture of the object.

2. Add lines and shapes to make natural patterns.

3. Redraw your lines with glue to add texture. Let your drawing dry and fill in the shapes with color.

 **Art Criticism**

Describe What object from nature did you draw?

Analyze What motif did you repeat to create your pattern?

Interpret Give your work a title.

Decide If you were making another natural pattern, how would you change your motif?

▲ **Peggy Flora Zalucha.**
(American). *Peony Blooms*
(IX). 1992.
....
Watercolor on paper. 44 × 68
inches (111.76 × 172.27 cm.).
Courtesy of Peggy Flora Zalucha.

Look at the two paintings. Both show objects that are repeated. When an object is repeated, this creates **rhythm.** Rhythm leads your eyes through a work of art.

 Art History and Culture

These paintings were made almost 100 years apart. What does this tell you about plants and people?

▲ **William J. McCloskey.**
Wrapped Oranges. 1889.

Oil on canvas. 12 × 16 inches
(30.48 × 40.64 cm.). Amon Carter
Museum, Fort Worth, Texas.

Study the two paintings to find their rhythm.

▶ What objects are repeated to create the rhythms in the two paintings?

▶ How does the positioning of the objects make your eyes move around the paintings?

Aesthetic Perception

Design Awareness Can you find examples of rhythm in the objects in your classroom? For example, pieces of chalk lined up are an example of rhythm.

Using Rhythm

When an artist draws an object, leaves space, and repeats the object, rhythm is created. The object is **positive space.** The empty space is **negative space.** Rhythm is made when an artist repeats a positive space and separates it with negative space. Can you find the positive space and negative space in this picture?

Practice

Create rhythm with your classmates.

1. Break up into small groups.

2. Arrange your group so you have rhythm.

3. Look at the other groups and their rhythm. Tell the other groups where your positive and negative spaces are.

◀ **Alvin Yu.**
Age 8.

Think about how this student used rhythm in his painting.

 Creative Expression

Can you create a still life using plants and rhythm? Paint a still life.

1. Choose and draw a plant. Repeat it several times to create rhythm.

2. Choose another object. Draw and repeat it as well.

3. Paint your composition.

 **Art Criticism**

Describe What plants did you use in your still life?

Analyze Where is the positive and negative space in your still life?

Interpret How did you create rhythm in your painting?

Decide How would your painting be different in you hadn't used rhythm?

Rhythm and Form

Look at the **storyteller doll** and the **diorama.** These pieces of art use forms, are three-dimensional, and have rhythm. Can you see the rhythm in these two sculptures?

◀ **Helen Cordero.** (Pueblo). *Storyteller Doll.* 20th century.
Museum of International Folk Art, Santa Fe, New Mexico.

 Art History and Culture

What do you think the inspiration was for these two works of art?

▲ **Vigil Family.** (Tesuque Pueblo). *Pueblo Scene: Corn Dancers and Church.* 1960.

Painted earthenware. Museum of International Folk Art, Santa Fe, New Mexico.

Study the two works of art to find examples of rhythm and form.

► What are the repeating objects in each work of art?

► How does looking at the repeating objects make your eye move through the art?

Aesthetic Perception

Design Awareness How could you arrange the items on your desk to create rhythm?

Using Rhythm and Form

Rhythm can also be made using forms. Artists who make sculptures or other three-dimensional art might include rhythm in their works to guide the viewer's eyes through their pieces. Like two-dimensional art with rhythm, artists use positive and negative space to create rhythm when using forms. Can you find the positive and negative spaces in the example below?

Practice

Create rhythm in an abstract sculpture.

1. Roll clay into a snake shape.
2. Make several balls of clay.
3. Place them on your snake to create rhythm using forms.

Think about how this student created rhythm in his storyteller doll.

◄ **Christopher Dominque.**
Age 7.

Creative Expression

Who would be your storyteller? Make your own storyteller doll.

1. Think of a person to be your storyteller.

2. Create a clay figure of this person. Add arms, legs, hands, feet, and any details you wish.

3. Make clay children and attach them to your storyteller.

4. Let your doll dry. Paint your doll with glazes to decorate it.

Art Criticism

Describe Who is your storyteller?

Analyze Which forms in your storyteller are used to create rhythm?

Interpret Where are the positive spaces and negative spaces that create rhythm in your work of art?

Decide Do you think it is easier to create rhythm using two- or three-dimensional objects?

Lesson 5 Diagonal Movement

Look how these works of art use rhythm and **diagonal movement.** The artists wanted viewers to feel the excitement of dancing. The bodies are placed to make your eyes move around the painting.

◄ **Thomas Hart Benton.** (American). *Country Dance.* 1929.

Oil on gessoed canvas. 30 × 25 inches (76.2 × 63.5 cm.). Private Collection.

 Art History and Culture

Look at the way people in the paintings are dressed. What does the music they are dancing to sound like?

▲ **Edgar Degas.** (French).
Ballet Scene. 1907.

Pastel on cardboard. 30 $\frac{1}{4}$ × 43 $\frac{3}{4}$
inches (76.84 × 111.13 cm.). National
Gallery of Art, Washington, D.C.

Study the two works of art to find examples
of diagonal movement.

▶ Where do you see diagonal lines in the two
pictures?

▶ What path do your eyes take as they move
around the pictures?

▶ Which painting has the fastest moving
people? Explain.

Aesthetic Perception

Seeing Like an Artist Name a time when people's
arms and legs move diagonally.

Using Diagonal Movement

Artists use rhythm to create **movement** in a work of art. Movement helps art seem alive and makes a viewer's eyes follow a path across the art. When artists use diagonal lines, the viewer's eyes follow a diagonal path. Use your finger to trace the path your eye follows while looking at this picture. Are you tracing diagonal lines?

Practice

Draw diagonal lines to match music.

1. Listen to the music that your teacher is playing.

2. Draw diagonal and zigzag lines on your paper to match the music.

3. Look for the diagonal movement in your drawing. How will your viewer's eyes move?

◀ **Becca Smith.**
Age 7.

Think about how this student made the trees dance in the wind.

Creative Expression

How could you show movement in a dance? Draw a dance scene using the computer.

1. Think about how your arms and legs move when you are dancing. How do objects dance in the wind?

2. Open your computer drawing program.

3. Draw a dance scene that shows lots of diagonal movement. Think about how you want your viewer's eyes to move across your picture.

Art Criticism

Describe Who or what is dancing in your picture?

Analyze Where are the diagonal lines in your picture?

Interpret Where is the diagonal or zigzag path in your drawing?

Decide What other activities would make good drawings for diagonal movement?

Curving Movement

▲ **Vincent van Gogh.**
(Dutch). *The Starry Night.*
1889.

Oil on canvas. 29 × 36 $\frac{3}{10}$ inches
(73.7 × 92.1 cm.). Museum of
Modern Art, New York, New York.

Look at these works of art. These two paintings were made using rhythm and many curving lines. Like diagonal movement, **curving movement** also can make your eyes move across a work of art.

Art History and Culture

Look at the two paintings. What do you think these places are like? Do you think they are real or imaginary?

▲ **David Hockney.** (English).
Garrowby Hill. 1998.

Oil on canvas. 60 × 76 inches (152.4 × 193.04 cm.). Museum of Fine Arts, Boston, Massachusetts.

Study the two works of art and find examples of curving movement.

▶ Where do you see curving movement in these two paintings?

▶ What paths do your eyes take as they move across the paintings?

Aesthetic Perception

Design Awareness Look at a map and trace several roads. What kind of movement did you find?

Using Curving Movement

Like diagonal movement, curving movement is made using rhythm. Curving movement draws the viewer's eyes across a work of art in curving lines. Artists use curving movement to make their work feel alive and exciting.

Where is the curving movement in the picture? Trace the curving movement with your fingers.

Practice

Draw a road using curving movement.

1. Think of a road.

2. Draw the road on your paper using curving movement.

3. What path does your road take across your paper? What do you think is at the end of your road?

◄ **Lauren Welch.**
Age 7.

Think about how this student used curving movement in her picture.

Creative Expression

If you were taking a journey, what kind of road would you take? Where would you go? Paint a picture using curving movement that shows your journey or place.

1. Think of a place you would like to visit or what the road there would look like.

2. Draw your road or place using curving and swirling lines.

3. Paint your place with watercolors.

Art Criticism

Describe What happens at your place or on your trip there?

Analyze Where are the curving lines in your painting?

Interpret What path do your eyes take when you look at your painting?

Decide What other kinds of scenes could you draw using curving movement?

Pattern, Rhythm, and Movement

▲ **Grandma Moses.** (American).
Grand Skating. c. 1946.

Galerie St. Etienne, New York, New York.

Art Criticism | Critical Thinking

Describe **What do you see?**

▶ How many people do you see? What are they wearing and doing?

▶ What animals do you see?

▶ Describe the rest of the scene.

Analyze **How is this work organized?**

▶ Where do you see curving movement? Diagonal movement?

▶ What shapes are repeated to form patterns?

▶ Where do you see people or objects repeated to create rhythm?

Interpret **What is the artist trying to say?**

▶ How does the rhythm and movement affect the feeling of this work? What is the mood of this work?

▶ Do you think this painting takes place in modern times or long ago? Why?

▶ If you could go into this painting, what sounds would you hear?

Decide **What do you think about the work?**

▶ Is this painting successful because it is realistic, because it is well organized, or because it has a strong message? Explain.

Show What You Know

Select the best answers to these questions. Write your answers on a separate sheet of paper.

1 A surface design made by repeating a motif is a _____.
A. rhythm
B. pattern
C. curving movement

2 _____ is the space between objects.
A. Negative space
B. Positive space
C. Motif

3 Artists use _____ to create movement in a work of art.
A. pattern
B. rhythm
C. positive space

4 Rhythm can be made using both _____ and _____.
A. motifs; patterns
B. curving movement; diagonal movement
C. shapes; forms

CAREERS IN ART
Movies

Did you know artists work on movies? Everything in a movie is made to look a special way.

CGI Animators draw pictures on a computer and animate them. CGI means *computer generated image.* Many movies are made using computers.

Art Directors help the director of a movie decide how the movie will look. They work with set designers, costumers, and lighting specialists to create the movie setting.

Set Builders build the scenery for a movie. Set builders might build one room or a whole city.

▲ **CGI Animator**

Pattern, Rhythm, and Movement in Storytelling

Geri Keams is a Navajo storyteller. She begins by singing a native song to the rhythm of a drum. *The Quillwork Girl* is a story she tells about a young Navajo girl with a talent for sewing porcupine quills onto buckskin. The adventure she has with her seven brothers is the Navajo legend of the creation of the Big Dipper. Cultures often use legends or myths to explain things in nature.

What to Do Retell a Native American legend or myth in your own words.

1. Work with three other students. Pick a legend and read it together.

2. List the main characters and words to describe them. Describe the setting of the legend.

3. Review the sequence of the legend.

4. Retell the legend. Create rhythm and movement by having one person start the legend, two people tell the middle, and one person tell the end.

▲ Geri Keams. "The Quillwork Girl."

Art Criticism

Describe Describe your favorite part of the legend.

Analyze How did you decide which was the beginning, middle, and end?

Interpret What feelings or moods were created as you told the legend?

Decide How well do you think your group did retelling the legend?

Balance, Emphasis, and Texture

▲ **Chryssa.** (American). *The Gates to Times Square.* 1966.
....
Welded stainless steel, neon, and
Plexiglas. 120 × 120 × 120 inches
(304.8 × 304.8 × 304.8 cm.). Albright-
Knox Gallery, Buffalo, New York.

Artists use the principles of balance and emphasis when arranging their work. Texture is an element that can be used to create emphasis.

This artist used **neon** to add emphasis to her art.

Artists use **balance** when putting together artwork. Balance makes the viewer feel that the work of art is well arranged.

▶ Does this sculpture have balance? Why or why not?

Artists use **emphasis** to call attention to parts of their art they want viewers to notice.

▶ What parts of this sculpture stand out?

Texture can be seen and felt. Texture is how things feel or would feel if they were touched.

▶ What would different parts of this sculpture feel like if you touched them?

In This Unit you will learn about and practice techniques to create balance, emphasis, and texture in your art. Here are the topics you will study:
▶ Balance
▶ Balance in People
▶ Emphasis
▶ Emphasis Using Contrast
▶ Tactile Texture
▶ Visual Texture

Chryssa

(1933–)

Chryssa was born in Athens, Greece, and moved to New York City in 1955. Chryssa loved the bright lights and activity that she saw in New York City. She started using neon in her art to try to capture the feelings she had when she looked at the big bright signs at night. She often uses letters or variations on letters in her art. *The Gates to Times Square* is one of the most important American sculptures.

Look at these two jars. Trace them with your fingers. Are the forms the same on both sides? When things are the same on both sides, they have balance and **symmetry.**

◄ **Artist Unknown.** (China). *Gui Ritual Food Container.* Zhou Dynasty, 11th century B.C.
....
Bronze. Arthur M. Sackler Gallery, Smithsonian Institution, Washington, D.C.

 Art History and Culture

What do you think people stored in these containers?

Study the two containers to find the balance.

▶ Describe the shape of each jar.

▶ How are the shapes of the forms the same on both sides of the jars?

◀ **Attributed to the Amasis painter.**
(Greek). *Lekythos (oil flask).*
c. 550–530 B.C.
....
The Metropolitan Museum of Art, New York, New York.

🔍 **Aesthetic Perception**

Design Awareness Look at containers in the classroom and at home that you use to store things. Do these containers have balance? Why do you think so?

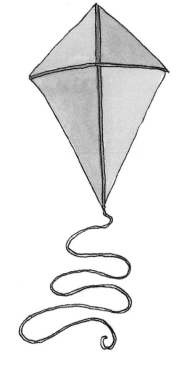

Using Balance

Balance happens when equal or similar shapes or objects are placed on opposite sides of an **axis.** An axis is a real or imaginary line across the center of the work of art.

Symmetry is a special type of balance. When art has symmetry, the two halves are mirror images of each other. Can you find balance in these pictures? Are they **symmetrical?**

Practice

Can you figure out if shapes are symmetrical?

1. Break into small groups.

2. Look at the selection of shapes your teacher has given you.

3. Find the axis of each shape. Decide if the shape is symmetrical. Share your results with the class.

◀ **Amber Mooney.**
Age 8.

Think about how this student used balance in her jar.

Design a symmetrical jar.

1. Think about the jar you want to make.

2. Fold a sheet of paper in half. Draw and cut out your jar shape. Glue your jar to your background paper.

3. Cut out small matching shapes. Arrange the shapes symmetrically around the axis and glue the shapes to the jar.

Describe What did you design your jar to hold?

Analyze Where is the axis of your jar?

Interpret How would your jar be different if you had not used symmetry?

Decide How could you design your jar so it had balance but not symmetry?

Lesson 2 Balance in People

Look at these two works of art. Both of these works of art are of people. People have balance.

◀ **Duane Hanson.** (American).
Policeman. 1992–1994.
••
Bronze polychromed oil, mixed media with accessories. Hanson Collection, Davie, Florida.

 Art History and Culture

Why did the artists make art of these people? What about the art tells you that these people are heroes?

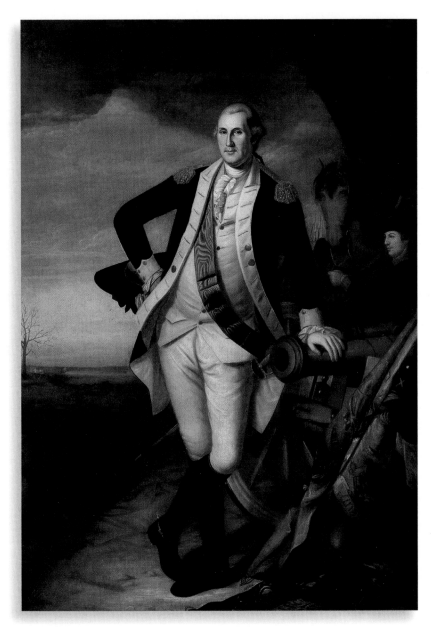

Study the two works of art of heroes to find balance in people.

▶ Can you find the axis in each person in each work of art?

▶ What body parts are repeated on both sides of the bodies?

◀ **James Peale.** (American). *George Washington.* c. 1782.

Oil on canvas. 36 × 27 inches (91.4 × 68.6 cm.). The Metropolitan Museum of Art, New York, New York.

Aesthetic Perception

Seeing Like an Artist Look closely at how people stand and sit. Do people tend to be in symmetrical or nonsymmetrical positions?

Using Balance in People

Art is not the only place you can find balance. People also have balance and symmetry. This means people also have an axis. Many body parts are mirrored on both sides of the body. Even though people have symmetry, they can be **posed** in ways so they are not symmetrical. Look at the pictures. Are both people symmetrical? Are both people balanced?

Practice

Can you draw people in symmetrical and nonsymmetrical poses?

1. Think of some poses.

2. Draw people in those poses.

3. Are all the poses symmetrical? Are all your people balanced?

Think about how this student used balance and symmetry in his hero picture.

◄ **Trent Abbey.**
Age 7.

Creative Expression

Who are some of your heroes? Draw your hero using balance and symmetry.

1. Think of a real or imaginary hero to draw.

2. Sketch your hero on your paper.

3. Use a black marker to outline your drawing. Add details using crayons, colored pencils, or markers.

Art Criticism

Describe Who did you select for your hero drawing?

Analyze Where is the axis in your hero drawing?

Interpret Why did you pick this person to be your hero?

Decide Do you like symmetrical or nonsymmetrical poses better for your hero drawing?

Emphasis

▲ **Lorenzo Scott.**
(American). *Ballet Dancers.*

Oil on canvas. 50 × 30 inches (127 × 76.2 cm.). Collection of Ann and Ted Oliver.

Look at these paintings. In both paintings, one person stands out from the other subjects. This is called emphasis. Artists have many ways to emphasize an object, including making it larger than other objects, using a different color, or using an unusual **point of view.**

 Art History and Culture

Look at the titles of these works. What do you think the relationships are among the people in these paintings?

Study the two paintings and look for emphasis.

▶ Which parts of the paintings look most important?

▶ How did the artists make parts of the paintings look more important?

▶ When you look at these paintings, what do your eyes move to first?

◀ **Cecelia Beaux.** (American). *Ernesta (Child with Nurse).* 1894.

Oil on canvas. $50\frac{1}{2} \times 38\frac{1}{8}$ inches (128.27 × 96.84 cm.). The Metropolitan Museum of Art, New York, New York.

Aesthetic Perception

Seeing Like an Artist Look at groups of people you see together. Does one person seem to stand out from the others?

Using Emphasis

Emphasis makes one part of a work of art seem more important than the rest of the work. The part that is important is called **dominant.** The parts of a work of art that are not emphasized are **subordinate.** If artists emphasize an entire area instead of an object, they create a **focal point.**

Practice

Read a sentence aloud and give a word emphasis.

1. Look at the sentence your teacher gives you.

2. Pick a word to emphasize. When it is your turn, read your sentence aloud.

3. Have your classmates tell you which word you emphasized.

◀ **Ryan Spell.**
Age 7.

Think about how this student created emphasis in his drawing.

Creative Expression

Can you draw a group of people and give one person emphasis? Draw a picture of a group of people.

1. Think of a scene that shows people working or playing.

2. Draw the scene using markers. Give one person in the scene emphasis.

3. Color your picture and add details.

Art Criticism

Describe What are the people in your scene doing?

Analyze Who in your scene has emphasis?

Interpret How did you emphasize the person in your scene?

Decide What would your scene look like if there were no emphasis?

Emphasis Using Contrast

▲ **Rembrandt van Rijn.**
(Dutch). *The Mill.* c. 1650.
. . . .
Oil on canvas. $34\frac{1}{2} \times 38\frac{1}{8}$ inches
(87.63 × 96.84 cm.). The National
Gallery of Art, Washington, D.C.

Look at these two paintings. The artists used **contrast** to create emphasis and focal points in these paintings. Contrast occurs when two objects that are different are placed together. For example, a light color is placed next to a dark color.

 Art History and Culture

What kind of people do you think would live in these buildings?

◀ **Rene Magritte.** (Belgian).
The Empire of Lights. 1954.

Oil on canvas. $18\frac{1}{2} \times 24\frac{1}{8}$ inches
(46.99 × 61.28 cm.). Musees d'Art
Moderne, Brussels, Belgium.

Study these two paintings to find emphasis, focal points, and contrast.

▶ What areas of these paintings do you notice first?

▶ Which areas of the paintings are alike?

🔍 Aesthetic Perception

Design Awareness Look for things that stand out in your classroom because of contrast. For example, a shiny glass clock against a dull wall creates contrast.

Using Emphasis
Using Contrast

Contrast is a way to create a focal point. When an artist uses an object that is different from the other objects in an area, this creates contrast. Artists can create contrast by varying sizes of objects, types of shapes they use, hues of objects, or values of areas. What is creating contrast in the pictures below?

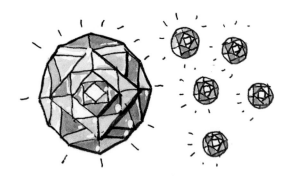

Practice

Draw two objects that contrast each other.

1. Choose a way to create contrast. Think of two objects to draw.

2. Draw the objects on your paper so they create contrast.

3. Explain to the class how you created contrast in your drawing.

◀ **Caleb Hudson.**
Age 7.

Think about how this student used contrast in his night scene.

 **Creative Expression**

Can you use contrast in a nighttime scene? Draw a building at night using contrast.

1. Think of a night scene to draw. Draw the scene on dark construction paper.

2. Add the contrast of lights in the dark by using yellow and white oil pastels.

3. Add details to your drawing and name it.

 **Art Criticism**

Describe What is happening in your nighttime scene?

Analyze Where are the focal points in your drawing?

Interpret Would your drawing still have contrast if you used light paper and dark pastels?

Decide How else could you have created contrast in your drawing?

Lesson 5 Tactile Texture

▲ **Jacob Gay.** (American). *Powder Horn.* 1759.

Cow horn. 15 $\frac{1}{2}$ inches (39.97 cm.). The Metropolitan Museum of Art, New York, New York.

Look at these two works of art. Notice the **carving** on the horn and the **stitchery** on the quilt. How do you think the quilt and the carved horn would feel if you touched them? The way things feel is called texture.

 Art History and Culture

Why do you think these artists used maps in their art?

Study the two works of art and look for tactile texture.

► What do you think the horn would feel like if you touched it?

► What do you think the quilt would feel like if you touched it?

▲ **Artist Unknown.**
(American). *Map Quilt.*
1886.
. . . .
Silk and cotton with silk embroidery.
78 $\frac{3}{4}$ × 82 $\frac{1}{4}$ inches (200.03 × 208.92 cm.). American Museum of Folk Art, New York, New York.

Aesthetic Perception

Design Awareness Why do you think some maps are designed with tactile texture? How would that help someone looking at the map?

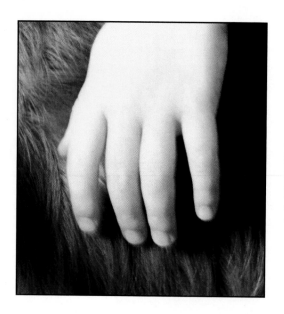

Using Tactile Texture

One way we identify texture is by touching it. Texture you can touch and feel is called **tactile texture.** Tactile texture can be **rough** or **smooth.** What are some words you would use to describe tactile textures?

Gather objects that have tactile texture.

1. Break into small groups.

2. Gather objects from the pile that are good examples of the tactile texture word your teacher gives you.

3. Share your word and objects with the rest of the class.

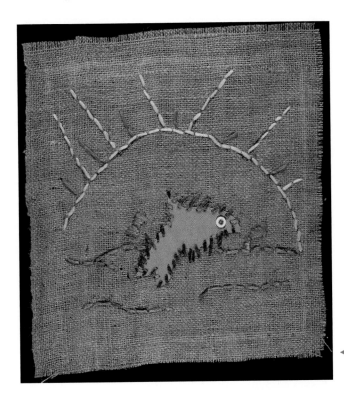

◀ **Veeda Mashayekh.**
Age 7.

Think about how this student used texture in her map decoration.

Creative Expression

How would you decorate a map? Sew a work of art to decorate a map using texture.

1. Think about a design you could make with fabric to decorate a map. Draw your ideas on fabric scraps.

2. Cut them out and stitch them onto your fabric background.

3. Add more details with stitches and buttons.

Art Criticism

Describe How did you construct your stitchery?

Analyze What textures does your stitchery project have?

Interpret How would your stitchery be different if you used materials with different textures?

Decide If you were going to make a stitchery map decoration again, what other items would you sew?

Visual Texture

Look at these two **portraits.** These artists used texture to paint their subjects' clothing. You can't touch the paintings and feel the texture of the clothes. What do you think the subjects' clothes would feel like if you could touch them?

◀ **Jan Vermeer.** (Dutch). *The Girl With the Red Hat.* c. 1665.
....
Oil on panel. $9\frac{1}{2} \times 7\frac{1}{8}$ inches (24.13 × 18.10 cm.). The National Gallery of Art, Washington, D.C.

 Art History and Culture

Look at the clothing in these paintings. When do you think these people lived? What do you think they did? Why?

◀ **George Catlin.**
(American). *NO-HO-MUN-YA, One Who Gives No Attention.* 1844.

Oil on canvas. 29 × 24 inches (73.66 × 60.96 cm.). Smithsonian American Art Museum, Washington, D.C.

Study the two portraits to find examples of visual texture.

▶ What would the girl's hat feel like?

▶ What would the man's necklace feel like?

Aesthetic Perception

Seeing Like an Artist Look around at the different textures in the room. How does light reflect off of the different textures?

Using Visual Texture

Visual texture is texture you see. Artists use visual texture to describe how something feels when the viewer can't touch the object. Visual texture is created by copying the way light reflects off of different surfaces. Surfaces can be **shiny** or **matte.** Look at the picture. Even though you cannot touch the object, you can describe how it would feel.

Practice

Can you capture visual textures? Make rubbings of visual textures.

1. Choose several different textures from the selection your teacher has.

2. Place your paper on top of a textured surface. Use the long side of your crayon to make a rubbing.

3. Look at the different rubbings you made. Save them for later use.

◀ **Clayton Beahr.**
Age 7.

Think about how this student used visual textures in his collage.

 **Creative Expression**

How would you use visual textures to design clothing? Create a collage.

1. Draw items of clothing on the visual textures you collected.

2. Cut out the clothes and glue them onto your paper.

3. Use markers to draw people wearing the clothes.

 **Art Criticism**

Describe What kind of clothes are the people in your collage wearing?

Analyze What different visual textures did you use for your clothing?

Interpret How do you want your viewers to feel about the clothes you created?

Decide Would you like to wear clothes that feel the way your textures do?

Balance, Emphasis, and Texture

▲ **Rosalind Ragans.** (American). *Teacher.* 1988.

Batik dyes and wax on cotton fabric. 27 × 23 inches (68.58 × 58.42 cm.). Private Collection.

Art Criticism | Critical Thinking

Describe **What do you see?**

▶ What do you see in this painting?

Analyze **How is this work organized?**

▶ Which part of this work shows balance?

▶ Is the texture in this art visual or tactile? Describe it.

▶ What part of this work shows emphasis?

Interpret **What is the artist trying to say?**

▶ Whose face is this?

▶ What is happening in this picture? Tell the story you see.

Decide **What do you think about the work?**

▶ Is this painting successful because it is realistic, because it is well organized, or because it has a strong message? Explain your answer.

Balance, Emphasis, and Texture, continued

Show What You Know

Answer these questions on a separate sheet of paper.

1 Visual texture is texture you _____.
   A. see
   B. touch
   C. balance

2 _____ occurs when two sides of a work of art are mirror images.
   A. Visual texture
   B. Emphasis
   C. Symmetry

3 _____ makes one part of a work of art stand out.
   A. Balance
   B. Emphasis
   C. Symmetry

4 _____ occurs when two different objects are placed next to each other.
   A. Tactile texture
   B. Balance
   C. Contrast

VISIT A MUSEUM
The National Gallery of Canada

The National Gallery of Canada was started in 1880 when members of the Royal Canadian Academy agreed to donate art to make a collection. At first the collection was in the same building as the Canadian Supreme Court. Soon the collection grew, and art was purchased for the museum. Today the collection has a permanent home in Ottawa, and the museum occupies over 500,000 square feet.

Balance, Emphasis, and Texture in Dance

Remey Charlip is a choreographer who finds new and interesting ways to create dances. Instead of making up specific dance steps, he thinks of everyday movements and changes them to fit into the dance. When people dance, they emphasize the way they are moving and the rhythm of their movements. Remey Charlip makes up his dances by emphasizing everyday movements.

What to Do Create a Radio Dance using contrasting movements.

1. Make up a Radio Dance with a small group. Brainstorm and select five or seven common action words and place them in an order. Examples of some action words are *stretch, turn, toss, jump,* and *swing.* Decide which movements will have more emphasis.

2. Select an announcer to call out the words while the rest of the group improvises ways to change an ordinary movement into a dance. The announcer should call "freeze" at the end of each movement.

3. Practice your Radio Dance several times. Perform it for the rest of the class.

▲ Remy Charlip. "Radio Dance."

 **Art Criticism**

Describe What did you do to turn a simple movement into a dance?

Analyze How did you give emphasis to one of your action words?

Interpret What feelings or ideas were you thinking of as you performed your dance?

Decide How well do you think your group did when you created a Radio Dance?

Harmony, Variety, and Unity

▲ **Diego Velázquez.** (Spanish).
Las Meninas (The Maids of Honor). 1656.
· ·
Oil on canvas. 10 feet 5 $\frac{1}{4}$ × 9 feet $\frac{3}{4}$
inches (3.18 × 2.76 meters). Museo
Nacional del Prado, Madrid, Spain.

Artists use harmony, variety, and unity to organize the elements of art.

When used correctly, harmony, variety, and unity make a work of art more interesting and pleasing to the viewer.

Harmony is the use of similar and related objects.

▶ Where are objects that are alike in this painting?

Variety is the use of different objects.

▶ Where are two objects that are different in this painting?

Unity occurs when artists balance harmony and variety.

▶ How do you feel when you look at this scene?

In This Unit you will learn about and practice creating harmony, variety, and unity. Here are the topics you will study:

▶ Harmony of Color
▶ Harmony of Shape and Form
▶ Variety of Color
▶ Variety of Shape and Form
▶ Unity in Sculpture
▶ Unity in Architecture

Detail from Las Meninas

Diego Velázquez
(1599–1660)

Diego Velázquez was the court painter for King Philip IV of Spain. He was famous for creating art that had unity. *Las Meninas* is one of Velázquez's most famous paintings. As court painter, it was his job to paint the scenes and people of the court. This painting shows the daughter of the king of Spain. If you look carefully, you can see her parents reflected in a mirror at the back of the painting.

Harmony of Color

Look at the two paintings. In each painting, one hue has been used to make many objects. By using the same hue for the different objects, the artists have made the viewer feel like these different objects belong together.

◀ **Paul Klee.** (Swiss).
The Tree of Houses. 1918.
. . . .
Watercolor and ink on chalk-primed gauze on papers, mounted on painted board. Norton Simon Museum, Pasadena, California.

 Art History and Culture

Colors represent different things in different cultures. Why do you think these artists chose red and green for their paintings?

▲ **Ivan Eyre.** (Canadian).
Valleyridge. 1974.
....
Acrylic on canvas. 50 $\frac{1}{10}$ × 64 inches
(142.4 × 162.6 cm.). National Gallery
of Canada, Ottawa, Canada.

Study the two works of art to find examples
of harmony of color.

▶ What is the main hue in each painting?

▶ Which objects in each painting are shades
or tints of the main hue?

▶ How does the artists' use of a main hue
make you feel about the scenes?

Aesthetic Perception

Seeing Like an Artist Look around the room and
find objects that are in the same color family. Do these
similar color groups create pleasant relationships?

Using Harmony of Color

Artists create **harmony** by making separate objects in a work of art look pleasing together. One way to create harmony is with color. When the same color is used for different objects or parts in a work of art, the viewer feels like the objects belong together. Look at the pictures. Which is more harmonious?

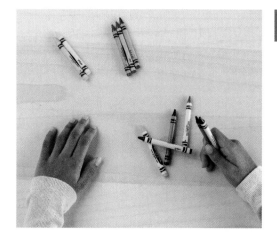

Practice

Group objects to create harmony of color.

1. Look at the crayons your teacher has given you.

2. Place the crayons in groups according to color families.

3. Can you see the harmony of color between the different crayons in each family?

◀ **Duncan Creek Second Grade.**
Ages 6–8.

Think about how these students used harmony of color in their tile mural.

Creative Expression

Can you use color to create harmony? Use color to harmonize a class mural.

1. As a group, decide on a theme and color for your class mural.

2. Paint the basic shapes of your design on your tile and let it dry. Remember to use the color your class selected.

3. Add details to your design. When the tiles are all dry, arrange them as a class.

Art Criticism

Describe What is the theme of your mural?

Analyze How did you create harmony of color in your mural?

Interpret How does your color choice help communicate your mural theme?

Decide Did you successfully create harmony using color in your mural?

Harmony of Shape and Form

▲ **Nuna Taqialuk.** (Inuit).
Polar Bears and Cubs.

· ·

7 × 12 × 9 inches (17.78 ×
30.48 × 22.86 cm.). Burdick
Gallery, Washington, D.C.

Look at these works of art. One is a sculpture and one is a painting. Both works of art create harmony using either shape or form.

 Art History and Culture

Why do you think these artists chose to create art using groups of animals? Why these animals?

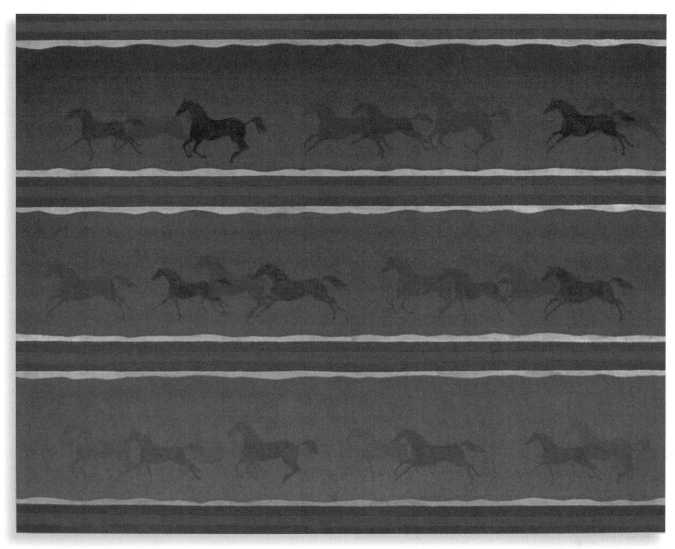

▲ **Paul Brach.** (American). *Red Horse Frieze.* 1983.

Oil on canvas. 54 × 72 inches (137.16 × 182.88 cm.). Collection of the artist.

Study the two works of art to find examples of harmony using shape and form.

▶ How many of each animal do you see in each work of art?

▶ How are the animals in each work of art similar?

Aesthetic Perception

Seeing Like an Artist Can you think of times when you have seen groups of animals? Why might animals be in a group together?

Using Harmony of Shape and Form

Harmony can also be created in a work of art using similar shapes and forms. When artists repeat shapes and forms that are related, they create harmony in their art. The shapes and forms may have different **proportions** and still create harmony. Look at the pictures. Which is more harmonious? Why?

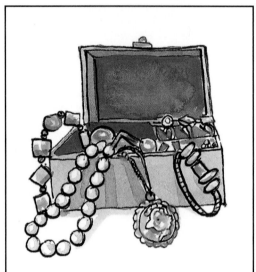

Practice

Draw a group of animals that has harmony.

1. Think of a group of animals to draw.

2. Draw them on your paper.

3. Why does your group have harmony?

Think about how this student used shapes to create harmony.

🎨 Creative Expression

Can you create a family of animals? Use the computer to draw an animal family.

1. Draw the adult animal or animals using the drawing tool.

2. Select and copy the adult animal several times. Resize the copies to create child animals.

3. Use the fill tool or drawing tool to add details to your animals.

⚠️❓ Art Criticism

Describe What animal did you use to create your animal family?

Analyze Why does your animal family have harmony?

Interpret What does the animal family that you created mean to you?

Decide If you were making another animal family, how else could you create harmony?

Variety of Color

▲ **Leo Lionni.** (Dutch).
Selection from Swimmy.
1963.

Look at the two works of art. Both are scenes of the sea and use many different colors. These artists used different colors to add interest to their works of art. In the *Swimmy* painting, one fish is a different color. In the Monet painting, the ocean is made of many different colors.

 Art History and Culture

Why did these artists paint pictures of the ocean? What do you think the ocean meant to them?

▲ **Claude Monet.** (French).
The Cliff, Etretat, Sunset.
1883.

Oil on canvas. 21 $\frac{3}{8}$ × 31 $\frac{3}{4}$ inches (55.3 × 80.7 cm.). North Carolina Museum of Art, Raleigh, North Carolina.

Study both works of art to find examples of variety of color.

▶ How many different colors do you see in these works of art?

▶ How did Leonni and Monet use colors to create difference and interest?

Aesthetic Perception

Design Awareness What would your classroom look like if everything in it were the same color? How would that make you feel?

Using Variety of Color

Artists use contrast to create **variety** in their art. Variety makes art more interesting. One way artists can create variety is by using different colors in a work of art. Look at the groupings. Which one has variety because of color?

Create a construction paper squid using variety of color.

1. Look at the picture of the squid your teacher has.

2. Draw a squid on construction paper. Cut your squid out.

3. Select an eye that will give your squid variety of color. Glue the eye on your squid.

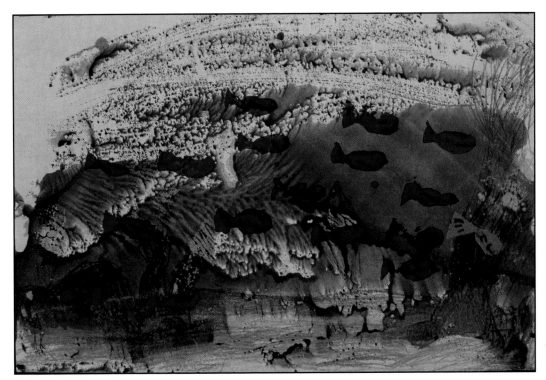

◄ **Mitchell Pettus.**
Age 7.

Think about how this student used variety of color in his underwater scene.

 **Creative Expression**

What do you think lives in the ocean? Make a print about ocean life.

1. Use crayons and draw the ocean floor on your paper.

2. To create the ocean, lightly apply paint to wet posterboard. Place your paper face down on the paint and rub your paper. Peel the paper away quickly.

3. Let your paper dry. Cut out construction paper sea creatures and glue them to your paper using variety of color.

 **Art Criticism**

Describe What animals live in your ocean?

Analyze Where did you create variety using color?

Interpret How does the variety of color make your ocean more interesting?

Decide What other scenes could you make using variety of color?

Look at these two birds. These artists used many different shapes and forms to make their works of art interesting. The swan is made of many different shapes. The eagle feathers are many different forms.

▲ **John James Audubon.**
(West Indian/American).
Tundra Swan. 1838.
•••••••••••••••••••••••
Historical Museum of Southern Florida.

 Art History and Culture

One bird is realistic, the other is not. Why do you think each artist made his bird in a different way?

▲ **Wilhelm Schimmel.**
(American). *Large Eagle.*

Paint on pine. 21 $\frac{3}{8}$ × 37 $\frac{3}{4}$ inches
(54.29 × 95.89 cm.). American
Folk Art Museum, New York,
New York.

Study the two works of art to find examples
of variety of shape and form.

▶ What different shapes do you see in
Tundra Swan?

▶ What different forms do you see in
Large Eagle?

🔍 Aesthetic Perception

Design Awareness Look at the art supplies in your
room. Where do you see variety of shape and form?

Using Variety of Shape and Form

Artists can create variety by using different shapes and forms in a work of art. By creating variety, artists can make their art more interesting to the viewer. If everything in a work of art were the same shape, the art would be **monotonous** and boring. Look at the pictures. Which one has more variety of shape?

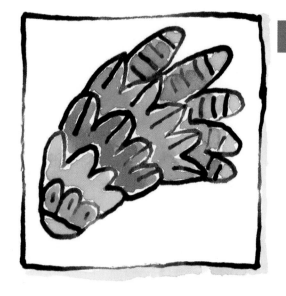

Practice

Draw the wing of a bird using variety of shapes.

1. Draw the wing of a bird.

2. Add feathers to the wing using different shapes.

3. Where are the different shapes on your wing? Did you create variety?

◄ **Rachel Yates.**
Age 7.

Think about how this student used variety of shape in her bird.

 **Creative Expression**

What kind of bid would you make? Create a fantasy bird using variety of shape.

1. Draw a fantasy bird. Make it large.

2. Outline your bird with black marker. Add pattern to your bird using black marker.

3. Use colored pencils to color the bird. Paint the background using watercolors.

 **Art Criticism**

Describe What does your fantasy bird look like?

Analyze How did you use different shapes to create variety on your bird?

Interpret How would your bird be different if you had not used variety of shape?

Decide Did the variety of shapes you used make your bird more interesting?

Unity in Sculpture

Look at these two works of art. One is a carousel. The other is a carousel animal. There are many different animals on the carousel, but when they are put together, they create one unified carousel.

◀ **Dentzel Company.** (American). *Carousel.* c. 1905.
• •
Ontario Beach, Rochester, New York.

 Art History and Culture

Many carousels were made using only horses. Why do you think this artist used so many different animals?

Study the two works of art to find examples of unity in sculpture.

▶ What kind of animals do you see on the carousel? Are they all the same?

▶ How do the animals on the carousel work together to make one object?

Aesthetic Perception

Design Awareness Look at a box of crayons. There are many crayons, but when put together they make one set. What other items do you see that make a set?

Using Unity in Sculpture

Artists balance variety and harmony to create **unity.** When a work of art has unity, the viewer feels like everything in the work of art belongs together and that nothing could be removed without changing the work of art. Unity brings all the elements in a work of art together. Look at the pictures. Which one has more unity?

Practice

Sketch objects that have unity.

1. Think of items that have unity, like a block of buildings, or a chest of toys.

2. Sketch one of these items on your paper.

3. What parts in your drawing come together to create unity?

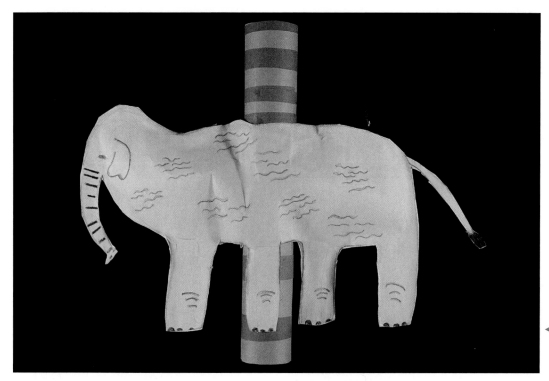

◄ **Rosemary
Ankerich.**
Age 7.

Think about how this student's animal
could be used to create unity in a carousel.

 **Creative Expression**

How would you create a class
carousel? Create a carousel animal.

1. Draw an animal. Add details and
paint the animal.

2. Cut the animal out and glue it to a
sheet of paper. Do not put glue
where the pole will go.

3. Stuff the animal with paper. Insert
the pole into the space left for it
and glue it in place.

4. Arrange your animals with your
class to create a carousel.

Art Criticism

Describe What type of
animal did you choose
and why?

Analyze What lines and
shapes did you use on
your animal?

Interpret What unifies
your class carousel?

Decide What other things
could you have done to
give your carousel unity?

Lesson 6 Unity in Architecture

▲ **Artist Unknown.**
(Roman). *Maison Carrée.* 1st century B.C.
....
Nimes, France.

Look at these two buildings. **Columns** go around the Roman temple to give it unity. Rodia combined many small towers and found objects to create unity in *Watts Tower*.

 Art History and Culture

What do you think these buildings were used for?

◀ **Simon Rodia.** *Watts Tower.*
1921–1954.

Steel rods, wire mesh, concrete, and found
objects. Watts, Los Angeles, California.

Study both works of art to find examples of
unity in architecture.

▶ What parts of each building are repeated?

▶ What similarities do you see in the forms in
these buildings?

Aesthetic Perception

Seeing Like an Artist Think of buildings that you
see in your community. What parts on the buildings
work together to create unity?

Using Unity in Architecture

Architecture is the study of buildings. When buildings are designed, **architects** decide how the parts of a building will work together to create one building. This gives the building unity. Look at this building. What parts work together to create unity?

Draw a building that has unity.

1. Think of different objects that you see on buildings.

2. Choose an object, and draw a building by repeating that object.

3. How does your building have unity?

Think about how this student created unity in his buildings.

 Creative Expression

How would you design a city? Draw a city that has unity using the computer.

1. Think of what your cityscape would look like.

2. Use the drawing tool and shape tools to make your buildings.

3. Add any details you wish.

Art Criticism

Describe Explain the design of your cityscape.

Analyze What parts of each building did you repeat?

Interpret How did you create unity in your cityscape?

Decide If you were going to design another cityscape, would you use unity?

Harmony, Variety, and Unity

▲ **Yvonne Jacquette.** (American). *Town of Skowhegan, Maine.* 1988.

Oil on canvas. 78 $\frac{3}{16}$ × 64 $\frac{3}{16}$ inches (198.60 × 163.04 cm.). Brooke Alexander Gallery, New York, New York.

Art Criticism · Critical Thinking

Describe **What do you see?**

▶ What kind of transportation do you see in this painting?

▶ What buildings do you see?

▶ Where else do you see objects made by people? What else do you see?

Analyze **How is this work organized?**

▶ Where did the artist create harmony using color and shape?

▶ Where did the artist create variety using color and shape?

▶ How did the artist create unity?

Interpret **What is the artist trying to say?**

▶ What part of town is shown?

▶ What is the difference between the cars close to the viewer and the cars at the top of the painting? Why are they different?

▶ Where do you think the artist was when she saw this scene?

Decide **What do you think about the work?**

▶ Is this painting successful because it is realistic, because it is well organized, or because it has a strong message?

Show What You Know

Write the best answers to these questions on a separate sheet of paper.

1. Artists create _____ by making different parts of a work of art pleasing to look at together.
   A. harmony
   B. variety
   C. monotonous

2. Adding _____ makes art more interesting to look at.
   A. paint
   B. harmony
   C. variety

3. Artists create _____ by balancing harmony and variety.
   A. architecture
   B. unity
   C. columns

4. _____ is the study of buildings.
   A. Architecture
   B. Variety
   C. Unity

Have you ever wondered why buildings look different? This is because of architecture.

Architects design all kinds of buildings. Architects think about how buildings will be used and what they will be made from.

Interior Designers design the inside of buildings. Interior designers select paint colors, furniture, fabrics, and the layout of the rooms.

▲ **Interior Designer**

Harmony, Variety, and Unity in Dance

▲ Korean Classical Music and Dance Company. "Korean Classical Music and Dance" and "Kahng Gang Sool Le."

The tradition of Korean folk music and dancing is very old. The music is played on stringed instruments, flutes, and different drums. The dancers wear bright costumes. The music and dancing show harmony and variety. When put together, they create unity.

What to Do Create a circle dance to a drum beat.

1. Stand in a circle with your classmates.

2. Create a dance by swaying and walking.

3. Add head movements, walking in a different direction, and raising and lowering your arms.

4. Perform your dance twice.

 **Art Criticism**

Describe Name the movements for your circle dance.

Analyze How is this dance similar or different to others you have done?

Interpret What feelings did you have as you performed your dance with others?

Decide How well do you think you did in performing a circle dance?

Technique Tips
Drawing

Pencil Basics

For darker values, use the side of your pencil lead, press harder, and go over areas more than once. You can add form to your objects using shading.

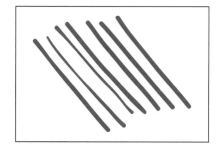
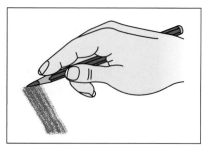
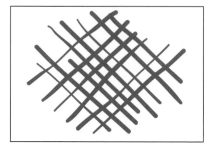

Colored Pencils

You can blend colors with colored pencils. Color with the lighter hue first. Gently go over the light hue with the darker hue until you get the hue you want.

You can create shadows by blending complementary colors.

Technique Tips

Crayon Basics

Crayons can be used to make thick and thin lines and dots. You can use both ends of a crayon.

You can color in large areas by using the long side of a crayon.

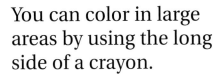

Marker Basics

You can use the point of a marker to create thin lines and small dots.

You can use the side of a marker tip to make thick lines.

Always replace the cap of a marker when you are finished using it.

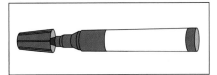

Technique Tips

Oil Pastels

Oil pastels can be used like crayons. When you press down hard on oil pastels, your picture will look painted. Oil pastels are soft and break easily. They can also be messy. Wash your hands with soap and water after using them.

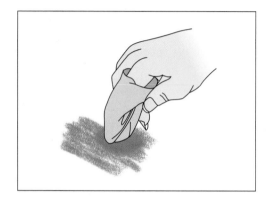

Colors can be mixed or blended by smearing them using a tissue or your finger.

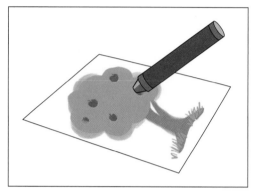

You can use oil pastels to draw over other media, such as tempera and crayon.

Colored Chalk

Colored chalks can be used to make colorful, soft designs. Colored chalk is soft and breaks easily. Reuse broken pieces.

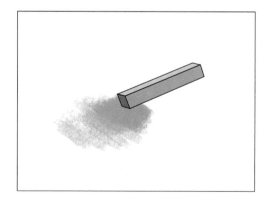

Make bolder colors by going over an area more than once.

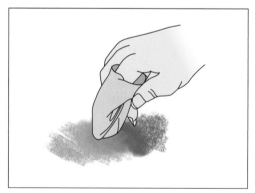

Blend colors by using a soft tissue or your finger.

Technique Tips

Painting

Brush Care

Rinse your brush in water between colors.
Blot the brush dry on a paper towel.

Clean the brush when you are finished painting.

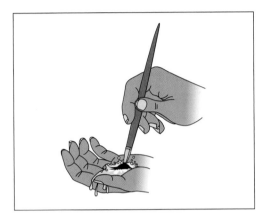

1. Rinse the brush in clean water. Wash the brush with soap.

2. Rinse the brush well again and blot it dry.

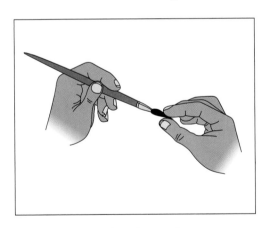

3. Shape the bristles.

4. Store brushes with bristles up.

Technique Tips

Tempera

Wet your brush in a water container. Wipe off extra water using the inside wall of the container and blot the brush on a paper towel.

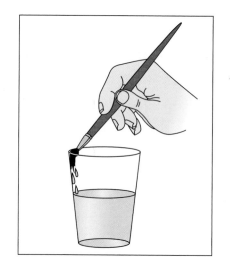

Mix colors on a palette. Put some of each color that you want to mix on the palette. Add darker colors a little at a time to lighter colors. To create a tint, mix a small amount of a hue into white. To create a shade, mix a small amount of black into a hue.

Use a thin, pointed brush to paint thin lines and details.

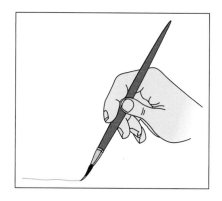

Use a wide brush to paint large areas.

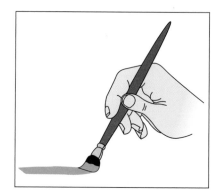

Technique Tips

Watercolors

Wet your brush in a water container. Wipe off extra water using the inside wall of the container and blot the brush on a paper towel. Add a drop of water to each watercolor cake. Rinse your brush between colors.

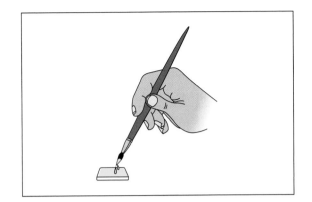

Mix colors on a palette. Put some of each color that you want to mix on the palette. Add darker colors a little at a time to lighter colors. To create a tint, add more water to a hue. To create a shade, mix a small amount of black into a hue.

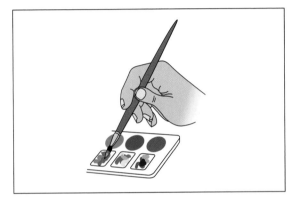

Paint on damp paper to create soft lines and edges. Tape your paper to the table, brush clean water over the paper, and allow the water to soak in.

Paint on dry paper and use very little water to create sharp lines and shapes.

Technique Tips

Watercolor Resists

Certain materials will show through water-colors. Crayons and oil pastels both show through watercolors. To make a watercolor resist, make a drawing using crayons or oil pastels. Then paint over the drawing using watercolors. The watercolors will cover the blank parts of the paper. The watercolors will not be visible on the parts of the paper covered with crayon or oil pastels.

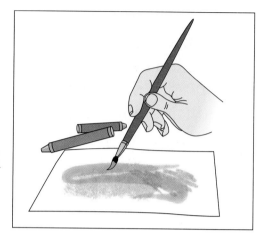

Collage

Scissors

Always cut away from your body.

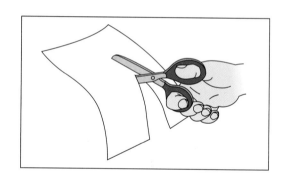

Ask a classmate to stretch yarn or fabric as you cut.

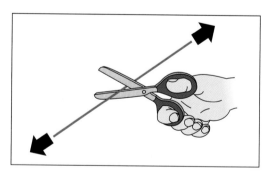

Use folded paper to cut symmetrical shapes. Fold a sheet of paper in half. Cut a shape using the folded edge as the axis.

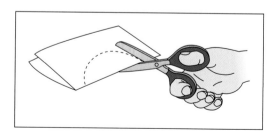

Technique Tips

Arranging a Design

When creating a collage, it is important to plan your design. Take into consideration the size of shapes and spaces, placement of shapes and spaces, color schemes, and textures. When you have made an arrangement you like, glue the shapes in place.

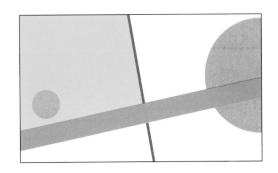

Glue

Squeeze a line of glue onto the paper. You can smooth the line with the tip of the glue bottle.

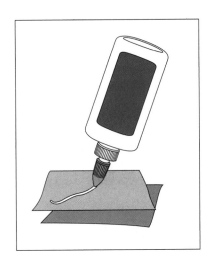

Close the glue bottle and clean the top when you are finished using it.

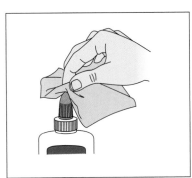

Technique Tips

Texture Rubbing

Place a texture plate or textured surface underneath your paper.

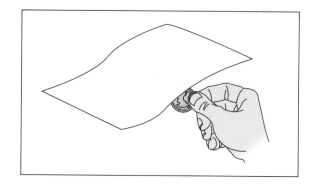

Hold the paper and object down firmly so they do not slip.

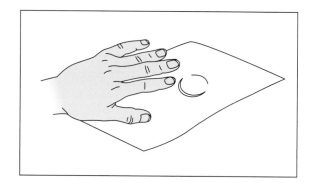

Use the long side of your crayon and rub away from you only. Do not move the crayon back and forth.

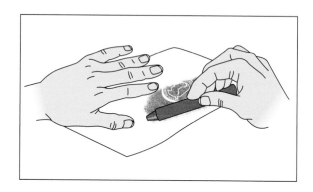

Technique Tips

Printmaking
Making Stamps

You can cut sponges into shapes to make stamps.

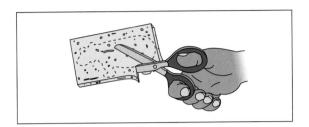

You can carve shapes into potatoes to make stamps.

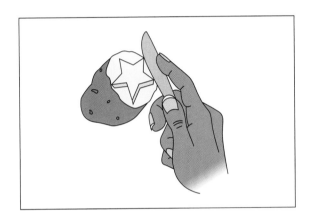

Making a Sponge Print

Use a different sponge for each color. Dip a sponge into paint. Press the sponge onto paper.

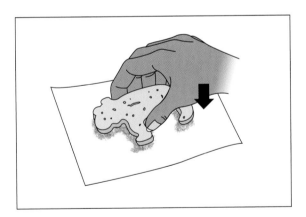

Technique Tips

Printing Stamps

Put a small amount of ink or paint on a flat solid surface. Roll a brayer back and forth in the ink until there is an even coating of ink on the surface and the brayer.

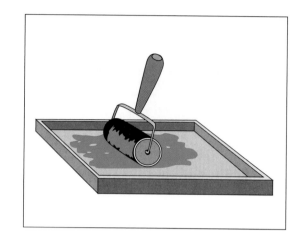

Roll the brayer over your stamp.

Apply the stamp carefully to your paper.

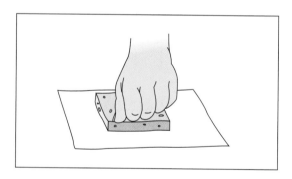

Technique Tips

Sculpture

Clay Basics

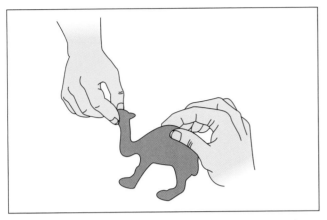

Clay can be pinched, pulled, and squeezed into the desired shape.

Store clay in an airtight container to keep it from drying out.

Pinch Pots

Push your thumb into your clay up to the first joint. Turn the clay on your thumb to create an opening.

Keeping your thumb in the hole, place your fingers on the outside of the clay and gently squeeze as you turn. Repeat until you have formed a bowl.

Gently tap the bottom of your bowl on your table so that it sits flat.

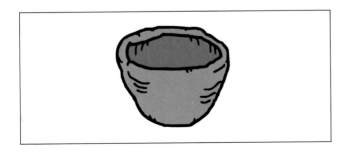

Technique Tips

Joining Clay

Two pieces of clay can be joined together by using slip and scoring.

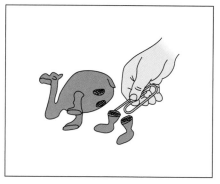

Score both pieces to help them stick together.

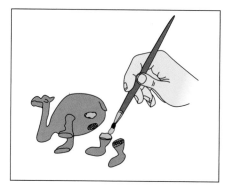

Apply slip to one of the pieces using a brush.

Squeeze together the two pieces of clay. Smooth the edges where they are joined.

Painting Clay

Clay can be painted and decorated with glazes once it is dry or fired.

Technique Tips

Paper Sculpture

You can curl, fold, and bend paper strips to make paper sculptures.

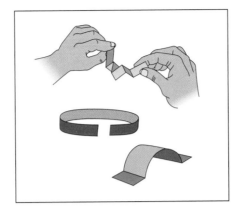

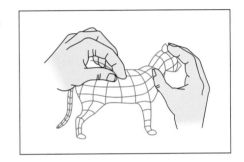

Papier-Mâché

Create a supporting form, if needed. Forms can be made of almost anything. Masking tape can be used to hold the form together.

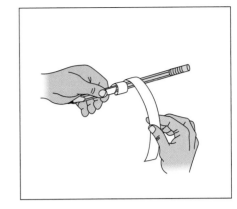

Tear paper into strips. Dip the strips into paste, or rub the paste onto the strips using your fingers. Use wide strips for wide forms and small strips for small forms.

Apply several layers of strips, applying each layer in a different direction. Smooth over rough edges with your fingers. When your sculpture dries, you can paint it.

Technique Tips

Aluminum Foil

Foil can be pinched and squeezed to make sculptures.

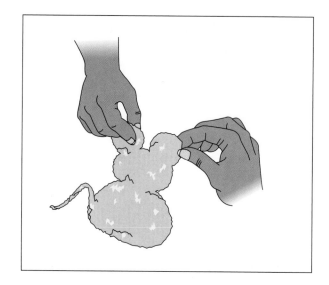

Building with Forms

To make sculptures with paper or cardboard forms, place the forms together and use masking tape to join them.

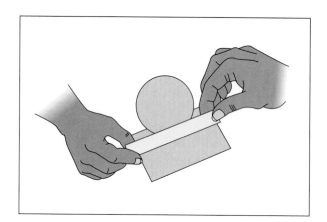

Technique Tips

Puppets

Cut out the pieces for your
puppet from paper.

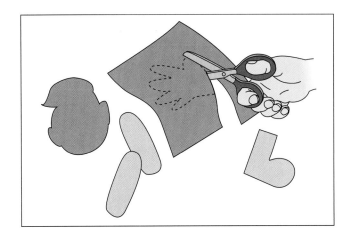

Use a hole punch to make holes
at the joints where two pieces
go together.

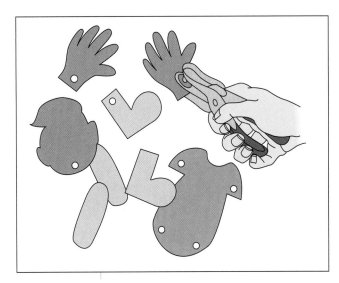

Use a brad to join the pieces.
Stick a brad through both holes,
and then unfold the metal clamps.

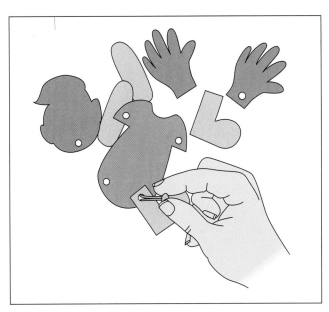

Technique Tips

Needlework

Thread your needle, or get help threading your needle. Tie a knot in the end of the thread.

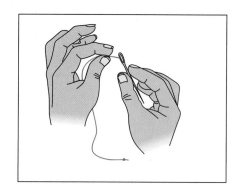

Carefully push the needle up from the bottom through the fabric where you want your stitch to start. Pull the needle through until the knot catches.

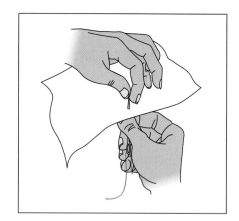

Carefully push the needle down through the fabric where you want your stitch to end. Repeat.

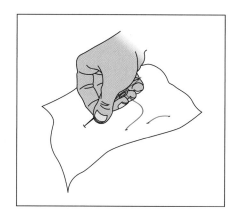

Technique Tips

Sewing a Book

1. Find the center of the fold and make a mark. Measure 1″ above and below the center mark.

2. Use a tapestry needle and poke holes through your marks.

3. Thread your needle and go through the top hole from the outside of your book and back through the center hole. Cut your thread so that you can tie both ends together.

4. Repeat for the bottom of your book.

Activity Tips

Line Direction

🎨 Creative Expression

1. Think of a playground you would like to create.
2. Twist, curl, and fold strips of paper to make different line directions.
3. Fold the ends of the strips for tabs and glue them onto the base paper to make your playground.

Types of Lines

🎨 Creative Expression

1. Draw the lines for your tree with a pencil. Fill the page.
2. Glue the line collage materials over the lines.
3. Add objects you like to the branches of the tree. Name your piece.

Activity Tips

Calm Lines

🎨 Creative Expression

1. Think of a calm water scene. What would you see there?

2. Paint your scene. Fill the paper using vertical and horizontal brush strokes.

3. Use markers to add details to your painting after it is dry.

Active Lines

🎨 Creative Expression

1. Think about which lines could describe an exciting event.

2. Draw different active lines with black paint to show the activity in your event.

3. Choose some bright colors and paint the spaces between the black lines.

Activity Tips

Unit 1 · Lesson 5 **Geometric Shapes**

🎨 **Creative Expression**

1. Think of a picture you would like to make.
2. Cut out geometric shapes using the colored construction paper.
3. Glue them onto the white paper to create your picture.

Unit 1 · Lesson 6 **Free-Form Shapes**

🎨 **Creative Expression**

1. Think of a puppet you would like to create.
2. Draw it and cut out the parts. Add any details to the parts that you wish.
3. Attach moving parts. Tape the puppet to a stick. Add a costume to the puppet using fabric and ribbon.
4. Hold the puppet in front of a light to make a shadow.

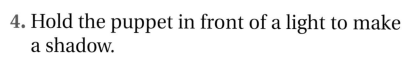

Activity Tips

Geometric Forms

 **Creative Expression**

1. Look at your teacher's selection of geometric forms. Think about how you would stack the forms. Plan your design.

2. Select three forms you want to work with. Stack and tape the forms.

Free-Form Forms

 **Creative Expression**

1. Think about things you like or that describe you. What free-form forms will you use to show these things?

2. Paint a background on tagboard.

3. Draw your forms on cardboard, decorate them, and cut them out.

4. Glue your free-form forms onto the background.

Activity Tips

Body Forms

🎨 Creative Expression

1. Decide how your body form will represent your culture.

2. Make the parts of your body form from the clay your teacher gives you. Join the pieces together using slip and scoring.

3. Add details to your body form by using a pencil to etch lines and shapes.

Animal Forms

🎨 Creative Expression

1. Think about a four-legged animal form you would like to make.

2. Create your animal form. Score your clay and use slip when joining two pieces.

3. Carve details in the clay.

Activity Tips

People and Space

🎨 **Creative Expression**

1. Think about the way your body moves when you play.

2. Use construction paper and draw a family playing. Cut out the shapes.

3. Arrange and overlap your family on white paper. Move them around until you like the way they look. Glue the shapes onto the paper.

- -

Objects and Space

🎨 **Creative Expression**

1. Think of some objects and foods you would like to draw.

2. Arrange your objects so some overlap.

3. Start by drawing the objects closest to you. Then draw the objects that are farther away.

4. Paint your still life.

Activity Tips

Unit 3 · Lesson 1 **Color and Hue**

 **Creative Expression**

1. Think of a scene or picture that you would like to draw.

2. Draw the scene on your paper using a black marker. Make your lines very bold.

3. Paint your picture using spectral colors in the correct order.

Unit 3 · Lesson 2 **Warm Hues**

 **Creative Expression**

1. Think of an object that reminds you of summer.

2. Draw that item with warm oil pastels.

3. Paint over the drawing using black tempera.

Activity Tips

Cool Hues

 **Creative Expression**

1. Think about your perfect backyard. What would it look like? What would be there?

2. Paint the background for your landscape using cool watercolors.

3. Add details to your painting using cool oil pastels or tempera paints.

Value

 **Creative Expression**

1. Think of an object that you see often in your neighborhood. Paint that object using white paint.

2. Mix black and white paint to create a gray value. Make a gray outline around your object.

3. Mix darker values and continue outlining your object until you make a black line.

Activity Tips

Light Values

🎨 **Creative Expression**

1. Pick three hues. Add small amounts of each hue to white to make tints.
2. Think about the scenery that people in the early American West would have seen.
3. Paint your picture using these tints.

Dark Values

🎨 **Creative Expression**

1. Choose a feeling that you would like to explain using pictures. Pick three hues to use.
2. Mix a small amount of black with each hue.
3. Paint your feeling picture using the shades.

Activity Tips

Unit 4 · Lesson 1   Patterns

 Creative Expression

1. Think of a motif that describes your culture. Draw the motif and cut it out of a sponge.

2. Dip your sponge into paint. Make prints on the paper using your motif to create a pattern.

3. Fill the paper with your pattern.

Unit 4 · Lesson 2   Patterns in Nature

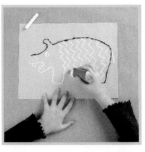

 Creative Expression

1. Think of an animal, plant, or other natural object. Draw a large picture of the object.

2. Add lines and shapes to make natural patterns.

3. Redraw your lines with glue to add texture. Let your drawing dry and fill in the shapes with color.

Activity Tips

Rhythm

Creative Expression

1. Choose and draw a plant. Repeat it several times to create rhythm.
2. Choose another object. Draw and repeat it as well.
3. Paint your composition.

- -

Rhythm and Form

Creative Expression

1. Think of a person to be your storyteller.
2. Create a clay figure of this person. Add arms, legs, hands, feet, and any details you wish.
3. Make clay children and attach them to your storyteller.
4. Let your doll dry. Paint your doll with glazes to decorate it.

Activity Tips

Diagonal Movement

Creative Expression

1. Think about how your arms and legs move when you are dancing. How do objects dance in the wind?

2. Draw a dance scene that shows lots of diagonal movement. Think about how you want your viewer's eyes to move across your picture.

Curving Movement

Creative Expression

1. Think of a place you would like to visit and what the road there would look like.

2. Draw your road or place using curving and swirling lines.

3. Paint your place with watercolors.

Activity Tips

Unit 5 · Lesson 1 **Balance**

🎨 Creative Expression

1. Think about the jar you want to make.
2. Fold a sheet of paper in half. Draw and cut out your jar shape. Glue your jar to your background paper.
3. Cut out small matching shapes. Arrange the shapes symmetrically around the axis and glue the shapes to the jar.

Unit 5 · Lesson 2 **Balance in People**

🎨 Creative Expression

1. Think of a real or imaginary hero to draw.
2. Sketch your hero on your paper.
3. Use a black marker to outline your drawing. Add details using crayons, colored pencils, or markers.

Activity Tips

Emphasis

🎨 **Creative Expression**

1. Think of a scene that shows people working or playing.

2. Draw the scene using markers. Give one person in the scene emphasis.

3. Color your picture and add details.

Emphasis Using Contrast

🎨 **Creative Expression**

1. Think of a night scene to draw. Draw the scene on dark construction paper.

2. Add the contrast of lights in the dark by using yellow and white oil pastels.

3. Add details to your drawing and name it.

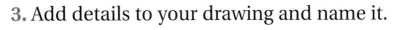

Activity Tips

Tactile Texture

🎨 Creative Expression

1. Think about a design you could make with fabric to decorate a map. Draw your ideas on fabric scraps.

2. Cut them out and stitch them onto your fabric background.

3. Add more details with stitches and buttons.

Visual Texture

🎨 Creative Expression

1. Draw items of clothing on the visual textures you collected.

2. Cut out the clothes and glue them onto your paper.

3. Use markers to draw people wearing the clothes.

Activity Tips

Unit 6 · Lesson 1 **Harmony of Color**

Creative Expression

1. As a group, decide on a theme and color for your class mural.

2. Paint the basic shapes of your design on your tile and let it dry. Remember to use the color your class selected.

3. Add details to your design. When the tiles are all dry, arrange them as a class.

Unit 6 · Lesson 2 **Harmony of Shape and Form**

Creative Expression

1. Draw the adult animal or animals using the drawing tool.

2. Select and copy the adult animal several times. Resize the copies to create child animals.

3. Use the fill tool or drawing tool to add details to your animals.

Activity Tips

Variety of Color

🎨 **Creative Expression**

1. Use crayons and draw the ocean floor on your paper.

2. To create the ocean, lightly apply paint to wet posterboard. Place your paper face down on the paint and rub your paper. Peel the paper away quickly.

3. Let your paper dry. Cut out construction paper sea creatures and glue them to your paper using variety of color.

Unit 6 · Lesson 4 **Variety of Shape and Form**

🎨 **Creative Expression**

1. Draw a fantasy bird. Make it large.

2. Outline your bird with black marker. Add pattern to your bird using black marker.

3. Use colored pencils to color the bird. Paint the background using watercolors.

Activity Tips

Unity in Sculpture

Creative Expression

1. Draw your animal on paper. Add details using oil pastels. Paint your animal using watercolors.

2. Cut your animal out and glue it to a sheet of paper. Do not put any glue at the places where the pole will go.

3. Stuff your animal with paper. Insert the pole into the space you have left for it and glue it in place.

4. Arrange your animals with your class to create a carousel.

Unity in Architecture

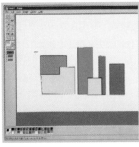

Creative Expression

1. Think of what your cityscape would look like.

2. Use the drawing tool and shape tools to make your buildings.

3. Add any details you wish.

Visual Index

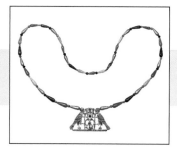

Artist Unknown
*Pectoral with the name
of Senwosret II*
c. 1897–1878 B.C.
(page 71)

Artist Unknown
Gui Ritual Food Container
11th century B.C. (page 156)

**Attributed to the
Amasis Painter**
Lekythos (oil flask)
c. 550–530 B.C.
(page 157)

Artist Unknown
*Maison Carrée,
Nîmes, France*
1st century B.C. (page 206)

Artist Unknown
*Plate with King
Hunting Rams*
late 5th century A.D.
(page 70)

Artist Unknown
Leopard Aquamanile
16th–19th century.
(page 79)

Louise Moillon
*Still Life with Cherries,
Strawberries, and Gooseberries*
1630. (page 87)

Rembrandt van Rijn
The Mill
c. 1650. (page 168)

Diego Velázquez
*Las Meninas (The
Maids of Honor)*
1656. (page 184)

Jan Vermeer
The Girl With the Red Hat
c. 1665. (page 176)

Maria Sibylla Merian
Plate 2 from "Dissertation in Insect Generations and Metamorphosis in Surinam"
1719. (page 130)

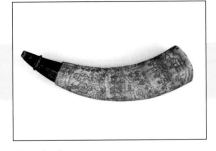

Jacob Gay
Powder Horn
1759. (page 172)

James Peale
George Washington
c. 1782. (page 161)

John James Audubon
Carolina Parakeet
1832. (page 131)

Artist Unknown
Princess Feather and Rising Sun
c. 1835–1845. (page 127)

John James Audubon
Tundra Swan
1838. (page 198)

George Catlin
NO-HO-MUN-YA, One Who Gives No Attention
1832. (page 177)

John Frederick Kensett
A View of Mansfield Mountain
1849. (page 105)

John Bell (attributed)
Figure of a Lion
c. 1850–1860. (page 78)

Artist Unknown
Delaware Shoulder Bag
c. 1860. (page 126)

Wilhelm Schimmel
Large Eagle
c. 1860–1890. (page 199)

Auguste Renoir
Two Sisters (On the Terrace)
1881. (page 83)

Claude Monet
The Cliff, Etretat, Sunset
1883. (page 195)

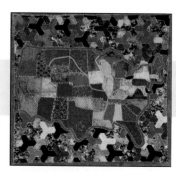

Artist Unknown
Map Quilt
1886. (page 173)

William H. McCloskey
Wrapped Oranges
1889. (page 135)

Vincent van Gogh
The Starry Night
1889. (page 146)

Cecilia Beaux
Ernesta (Child with Nurse)
1894. (page 165)

James J. Shannon
Jungle Tales
1895. (page 83)

Paul Cézanne
Still Life With Apples
1895–1898. (page 86)

Yoruba People
Headdress for Epa Masquerade
early 20th century.
(page 90)

Kiawak Ashoona
Seal Hunter
20th century. (page 75)

Helen Cordero
Storyteller Doll
20th century. (page 138)

Taqialuk Nuna
Polar Bears and Cubs
20th century.
(page 190)

Edward Steichen
The Flatiron
1904 (printed 1909).
(page 108)

Dentzel Company
Carousel
1905. (page 202)

Edgar Degas
Ballet Scene
1907. (page 143)

Claude Monet
Palazzo da Mula, Venice
1908. (page 45)

Robert Delaunay
Simultaneous Contrasts:
Sun and Moon
1913. (page 97)

Wassily Kandinsky
Composition VI
1913. (page 48)

Dentzel Company
Carousel Rabbit
c. 1915. (page 203)

Tom Thomson
Spring Ice
1916. (page 104)

Paul Klee
The Tree of Houses
1918. (page 186)

Joseph Stella
The Voice of the City of
New York Interpreted/ The
Great White Way Leaving
the Subway (White Way 1)
c. 1920–1922. (page 37)

Simon Rodia
Watts Tower
1921–1954. (page 207)

Georgia O'Keeffe
The Red Poppy
1927. (page 94)

Thomas Hart Benton
Country Dance
1929. (page 142)

Edward Hopper
Early Sunday Morning
1930. (page 53)

**Beatrice Whitney
Van Ness**
Summer's Sunlight
c. 1932–1934.
(page 101)

Minerva Teichert
Night Raid
c. 1935. (page 113)

Willam H. Johnson
Jitterbugs (II)
c. 1941. (page 60)

**Grandma Moses (Anna
Mary Robertson Moses)**
Grand Skating
c. 1946. (page 150)

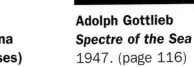

Adolph Gottlieb
Spectre of the Sea
1947. (page 116)

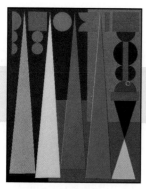

Auguste Herbin
Amour
1948. (page 52)

Henry Moore
Family Group
1948–1949 (cast 1950).
(page 64)

Artist Unknown
Indonesian Shadow Puppet
c. 1950. (page 56)

Ansel Adams
Early Sunday Morning, Merced River, Yosemite Valley, CA
c. 1950 (print c. 1978).
(page 109)

René Magritte
The Empire of Lights
1954. (page 169)

Harold Town
The First Aeroplane
1956. (page 117)

Franz Kline
Blueberry Eyes
c. 1959–1960.
(page 41)

Herón Martínez Mendóza
Church
c. 1960. (page 36)

Vigil Family
Pueblo Scene: Corn Dancers and Church
c. 1960. (page 139)

Jacob Lawrence
Street Scene (Boy with Kite)
1962. (page 34)

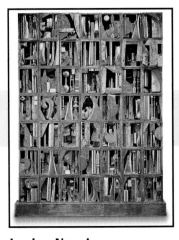

Louise Nevelson
Dawn
1962. (page 124)

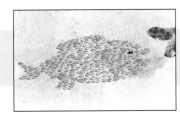

Leo Lionni
Selection from Swimmy
1963. (page 194)

David Smith
Cubi XVIII
1964. (page 63)

Artist Unknown
Thai Shadow Puppet
c. 1965. (page 57)

Chryssa
The Gates to Times Square
1966. (page 154)

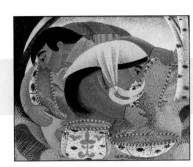

Patrick DesJarlait
Gathering Wild Rice
1972. (page 100)

Leo Twiggs
At Four and a Half
1972. (page 49)

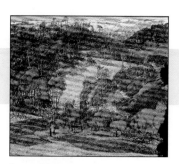

Ivan Eyre
Valleyridge
1974. (page 187)

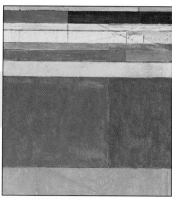

Richard Diebenkorn
Ocean Park #105
1978. (page 44)

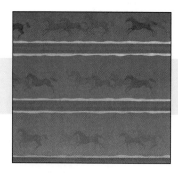

Paul Branch
Red Horse Frieze
1983. (page 191)

Robert Lostutter
Baird Trogon
1985. (page 96)

Miriam Schapiro
Personal Appearance
1985. (page 120)

John T. Scott
Alanda's Dream Tree
1985. (page 40)

Yvonne Jacquette
Town of Skowhegan, Maine
1988. (page 210)

Rosalind Ragans
Teacher
1988. (page 180)

Roxanne Swentzell
The Emergence of the Clowns
1988. (page 74)

Jane Wilson
Solstice
1991. (page 112)

Peggy Flora Zalucha
Peony Blooms IX
1992. (page 134)

Duane Hanson
Policeman
1992–1994. (page 160)

David Hockney
Garrowby Hill
1998. (page 147)

Jesús Moroles
Georgia Stele
1999. (page 67)

Lorenzo Scott
Ballet Dancers
2001. (page 164)

Glossary

A

active lines   Lines that show action and add energy and movement to a work of art. Diagonal, zigzag, and curved lines are examples of active lines.

angle   A shape formed when two lines extend in different directions from the same point

animal forms   A three-dimensional representation of an animal

arc   Any portion of a curved line from a circle

architect   Highly trained artists and engineers who design buildings

architecture   The study of buildings

axis   A real or imaginary line across the center of a work of art

B

balance   A principle of design that deals with arranging art. Balance occurs when equal or similar shapes or objects are placed on opposite sides of an axis in a work of art.

blob   A type of free-form shape

body forms   Three-dimensional representations of a person

brass   A metal made by combining copper and zinc

broken (line)   A line that is made of a series of dashes, not solid

C

calm lines   Lines that give a work of art a quiet and peaceful mood. Horizontal and vertical lines are calm lines.

carving Art made by cutting into the surface of the medium.

circle A round, geometric shape made when all points are placed the same distance from a center point.

coil A long roll of clay joined into a circle or spiral. Clay coils are used to make pottery.

color wheel A way of organizing the spectral colors in a circle

contrast A way of creating a focal point. Contrast occurs when elements that are different are placed next to each other in a work of art.

collage A work of art made of found objects, paper, or other things, glued on a surface

color An element of art that includes hue and value. Color refers to all the spectral colors as well as black and white.

column A supporting pillar on a building

cool hues Blue, green, and violet. Cool hues are associated with cool things like snow, water, and grass.

curved (line) A line that changes directions slowly and bends in arcs

curving movement Using curved lines to move the viewer's eyes through a work of art and make the viewer feel that objects in the work of art are moving along curves

D

dark value A value that has more black added to it

depth A front to back measurement, or how far back something goes

diagonal (line) A line that is oriented or moving on a slant

diagonal movement Using diagonal lines to move the viewer's eyes through a work of art and make the viewer feel that objects in the work of art are moving along diagonals

dimension A measurement of the amount of space an object takes up in one direction

diorama A display of a scene using sculpted, miniature, figurines

dominant The part of the work of art that seems more important to the viewer. Dominant elements have been emphasized.

E

earthenware Ceramics made out of clay and fired at a low heat

emphasis A principle of design that makes one part of a work of art seem more important than the rest

F

focal point An area of an artwork that has been emphasized

form Any object that has three dimensions: height, width, and depth

free-form form An irregular, three dimensional object

free-form shapes Irregular shapes. Splashes, blobs, and sails are all free-form shapes.

G

geometric forms A three dimensional object whose corresponding shape is geometric.

geometric shapes Common shapes that are regular, have specific names, and can be created using mathematical formulas. Circles, squares, triangles, and rectangles are all geometric shapes.

H

hand tools Simple instruments for carving or sculpting

harmony A principle of design that helps create unity by showing how objects in a work of art are similar

height A vertical measurement, or how tall something is

horizontal (line) Lines that are oriented or move from left to right.

hues The spectral colors, or colors of the rainbow. Hues do not include black or white. Hues are red, orange, yellow, green, blue, and violet.

I

irregular   Does not follow a rule or pattern

L

light value   A value that has more white added to it

line   A mark made by a tool, such as a pen, pencil, or crayon as it moves across a surface

M

matte   A visual texture that does not reflect much light

medium   The supply an artist uses to create art. Some mediums are clay, paint, or wood.

monotonous   Lack of variety; boring

motif   An image that is duplicated to create a pattern. Motifs can change color or position in a pattern.

movement   A principle of design that creates the feeling that objects in a work of art are changing position or are active

N

negative space   The empty space between and surrounding shapes and forms

neon   A special kind of light that can be made to be many bright colors

O

overlap   To place one object on top of another object and partially cover the first object up

P

painting   A picture or scene that an artist has created on canvas or another surface using paint

pattern   A decorative surface design. Patterns are two-dimensional. The part of the pattern that repeats is the motif.

photograph   A picture taken using light-sensitive film and a camera

point of view   The position from which the viewer sees an object or work of art

portrait   The image of a person, especially the face

posed   Arranged in a special way

positive space   Any shape or form

proportion   The relationship of the size of different objects to each other

primary hues   Red, blue, and yellow. Two primary hues mixed together make a secondary hue. No two colors can be mixed to make a primary hue.

print   An image created by using a stamp or printing plate. When artists make prints, they can make many identical images.

proportions   Size relationships between parts

R

rectangle   A four-sided geometric shape made of all right angles and whose opposite sides are equal in length.

relief   A type of sculpture where forms project from a flat background

rough   Tactile texture that feels uneven.

rough (line)   A line that has jagged, uneven edges

rhythm   A principle of design that is created by repeating objects through a work of art. Rhythm creates movement and is made by using positive and negative space.

S

sail   A type of free-form shape

sculpture   Three dimensional art that is not a body form

secondary hues   Orange, green, and violet. Two primary hues mixed together make a secondary hue.

shade   Dark value of a hue

shapes   A flat, two-dimensional figure. Shapes can only be measured by height and width.

shiny   A visual texture that reflects light well

smooth   Tactile texture that feels even

smooth (line)   A line that has even edges

solid (line)   A line that has no breaks, gaps, or holes

space An element of art that is the area in, around, and between objects. Shapes and forms are defined by the space around them.

spectral colors The hues in the rainbow or spectrum. Red, orange, yellow, green, blue, and violet.

spectrum The range of colors that it is possible to see; the rainbow

splash A type of free-form shape

square A four-sided geometric shape where all sides are the same length and all angles are right angles

statue Three dimensional art that is a body form

stitchery Technique for decorating fabric by sewing threads on it

storyteller doll A Native American sculpture that shows one person relating the history of the culture to many children

style A unique quality of an object

still life A painting or drawing of a collection of objects that cannot move

subordinate The parts of the artwork that seem less important. Subordinate objects are not emphasized.

symmetrical When two sides of a work of art are mirror images of each other

symmetry A special type of balance where two sides of a work of art are mirror images of each other

T

tactile texture The texture that can be felt

texture An element of art that refers to how things feel or would feel if they were touched

thick (line) Wide

thin (line) Narrow

three-dimensional Has measurements in three directions: height, width, and depth

tint A light value of a hue

triangle A three-sided geometric shape

two-dimensional Has measurements in two directions: height and width

U

unity The feeling that parts of an artwork belong together. Unity is created by balancing harmony and variety.

V

value How light or dark a color is

variety The use of different lines, shapes, and hues in artwork to create complicated relationships

vertical (line) Lines that are oriented or move up and down

visual texture Texture that can not be felt, but can be seen. Visual texture is often used in paintings.

W

warm hues Red, orange, and yellow. Warm hues are associated with warm things such as fire or sunshine.

width A horizontal measurement, or how long across something is

Z

zigzag (line) Diagonal lines that connect at their ends and change direction sharply

Index

A

Adams, Ansel, 109
Alanda's Dream Tree (Scott), 40
Amour (Herbin), 52
animals, 78–81
animators, CGI, 152
architects, 208, 212
architecture, 206–209
art directors, 152
Ashoona, Kiawak, 75
Audubon, John James, 131, 198
axis, 158, 162

B

Baird Trogon (Lostutter), 96
balance, 155–163
Ballet Dancers (Scott), 164
Ballet Scene (Degas), 143
Beaux, Cecilia, 165
Bell, John, 78
Benton, Thomas Hart, 142
Blueberry Eyes (Kline), 40, 41
body forms, 74–77
Brach, Paul, 191

C

careers, 92, 152, 208, 212
Carolina Parrakeet (Audubon), 131
Carousel Rabbit (Dentzel Company), 203
carving, 172
Catlin, George, 177

Cézanne, Paul, 87
CGI animators, 152
Chryssa, 154, 155
Church (Mendoza), 36
The Cliff, Etretat, Sunset (Monet), 195
colors, 94–107, 186–189
color wheel, 98, 102, 106
columns, 206
Composition VI (Kandinsky), 48
contrast, 168–171
Cordero, Helen, 138
Country Dance (Benton), 142
Cubi XVIII (Smith), 66
curators, 92

D

dance, 212
Dawn (Nevelson), 124
Degas, Edgar, 143
Delaunay, Robert, 97
Delaware Shoulder Bag (Unknown), 126
Dentzel Company, 203
depth, 88–89
DesJarlait, Patrick, 100
Diebenkorn, Richard, 44
dominant part, 166

E

Early Sunday Morning (Hopper), 53
Early Sunday Morning, Merced

River, Yosemite Valley, CA
(Adams), 108, 109
earthenware, 78
The Emergence of the Clowns
(Swentzell), 74
emphasis, 164–171
The Empire of Lights
(Magritte), 169
Ernesta (Child with Nurse)
(Beaux), 165
Eth-Noh-Tec, 93
Eyre, Ivan, 187

F

Family Group (Moore), 64
Figure of a Lion (Bell), 78
The First Aeroplane (Town), 117
The Flatiron (Steichen), 108
florists, 92
focal point, 166, 170
form
    and animals, 78–81
    body, 74–77
    defined, 64–65
    geometric, 66–69
    and harmony, 192–193
    and rhythm, 138–142
    and theater, 93
    three-dimensional, 68
    and variety, 198–201
At Four and a Half (Twiggs), 49
free-form forms, 70–73
free-form shapes, 56–59

G

Garrowby Hill (Hockney), 147

The Gates to Times Square
(Chryssa), 154, 155
Gathering Wild Rice
(DesJarlait), 100
Gay, Jacob, 172
geometric forms, 66–69
geometric shapes, 52–55
George Washington (Peale), 161
Georgia Stele (Moroles), 67
Girl With the Red Hat
(Vermeer), 176
Gottlieb, Adolph, 116
Grand Skating (Moses), 150
Gui Ritual Food Container, 156

H

Hanson, Duane, 160
harmony
    of color, 186–189
    in dance, 212
    defined, 185
    of shape and form, 192–193
Headdress for Epa Masquerade
(Yoruba People), 90
Herbin, Auguste, 52
Hockney, David, 147
Hopper, Edward, 53
hues, 94, 96–99, 100–107, 114,
    186–189

I

Indonesian Shadow Puppet
(Unknown), 56
interior designers, 212

J

Jacquette, Yvonne, 210
Jitterbugs [II] (Johnson), 60
Johnson, Willam H., 60
Jungle Tales (Shannon), 82

K

Kandinsky, Wassily, 48
Kensett, John Frederick, 105
Klee, Paul, 186
Kline, Franz, 41

L

Large Eagle (Schimmel), 199
Las Meninas (The Maids of Honor)
   (Velazquez), 184, 185
Lawrence, Jacob, 35
Leopard Aquamanile
   (Unknown), 79
light, 178
lines
      active, 48–51
      calm, 44–47
      and movement, 48–51
      types of, 40–43
      using, 34–39
Lionni, Leo, 194
Lostutter, Robert, 96

M

Magritte, Rene, 169
Maison Carree, Nimes, France
   (Unknown), 206
Map Quilt (Unknown), 173
matte surface, 178

McCloskey, William H., 135
Mendoza, Heron Martínez, 36
Merian, Maria Sibylla, 130
The Mill (van Rijn), 168
Moillon, Louise, 86
Monet, Claude, 45, 195
Moore, Henry, 64, 65
Moroles, Jesús, 67
Moses, Grandma, 150
motif(s), 126–129
movement, 48–51, 125, 142–149
The Museum of Modern Art, 122
museums, 62, 122, 182

N

National Gallery of Canada, 182
nature, 130–133
negative space, 136
neon, 154
Nevelson, Louise, 124, 125
Night Raid (Teichert), 113
*NO-HO-MUN-YA, One Who Gives
   No Attention* (Catlin), 177

O

Ocean Park #105 (Diebenkorn), 44
O'Keeffe, Georgia, 94, 95
overlapping, 82–85, 87

P

Palazzo da Mula, Venice
   (Monet), 45
pattern, 125–133
Peale, James, 161

Pectoral with the Name of Senwosret II (Unknown), 71

Peony Blooms IX (Zalucha), 134

people, 74–77, 82–85, 160–163

Personal Apperance (Schapiro), 120

photographs, 108–109

Plate 2 (from "Dissertation in Insect Generations and Metamorphosis in Surinam (Merian), 130

Plate with Rams (Unknown), 70

point of view, 164

Polar Bears and Cubs (Taqialuk), 190

Policeman (Hanson), 160

portraits, 176

positive space, 136

Powder Horn (Gay), 172

primary hues, 98

proportion, 192

Pueblo Scene Corn Dancers and Church (Vigil Family), 139

puppets, 56–59

R

Ragans, Rosalind, 180

rainbow colors, 94

Red Horse Frieze (Branch), 191

The Red Poppy (O'Keeffe), 94

reliefs, 70, 73

Rembrandt (van Rijn), 168

Renoir, Pierre Auguste, 83

rhythm, 125, 134–142

Rodia, Simon, 207

S

Schapiro, Miriam, 120

Schimmel, Wilhelm, 199

Scott, John T., 40

Scott, Lorenzo, 164

sculpture, 66–69, 78, 140, 202–205

Seal Hunter (Ashoona), 74, 75

secondary hues, 98

Selection from Swimmy (Lionni), 194

set builders, 152

shade, 118

Shannon, James J., 82

shape(s). *See also* form
free-form, 56–59
geometric, 52–55
and harmony, 192–193
irregular, 58
two-dimensional, 68, 128
and variety, 198–201

shiny surface, 178

Simultaneous Contrasts: Sun and Moon (Delaunay), 97

Smith, David, 66

The Smithsonian Museum of American Art, 62

Solstice (Wilson), 112

space, 82–89, 93, 136

Spectre of the Sea (Gottlieb), 116

spectrum, 94–95

Spring Ice (Thomson), 104

The Starry Night (van Gogh), 146

statues, 74–75

Steichen, Edward, 108

Steiglitz, Alfred, 95

Stella, Joseph, 37

still lifes, 86–89
Still Life with Apples
  (Cézanne), 87
Still Life with Cherries,
  Strawberries, and Gooseberries
  (Moillon), 86
stitchery, 172, 175
Storyteller Doll (Cordero), 138
Street Scene (Boy with Kite)
  (Lawrence), 34
subordinate part, 166
Summer's Sunlight
  (Van Ness), 101
Swentzell, Roxanne, 74
symmetry, 156, 158, 162

T

tactile texture, 173–174
Taqialuk, Nuna, 190
Teacher (Ragans), 180
Teichert, Minerva, 113
texture, 155, 172–179
Thai Shadow Puppet
  (Unknown), 57
theatre, 93
Thomson, Tom, 104
three-dimensional forms, 68, 140
tint, 114
Town, Harold, 117
Town of Skowhegan, Maine
  (Jacquette), 210
The Tree of Houses (Klee), 186
Tundra Swan (Audubon), 198
Twiggs, Leo, 49

two-dimensional shape, 68, 128
Two Sisters (On the Terrace)
  (Renoir), 83

U

unity, 185, 202–209, 212

V

Valleyridge (Eyre), 187
value, 108–109, 110–119
van Gogh, Vincent, 146
Van Ness, Beatrice Whitney, 101
van Rijn, Rembrandt, 168
variety, 185, 194–201, 212
Velásquez, Diego, 184, 185
Vermeer, Jan, 176
A View of Mansfield Mountain
  (Kensett), 104, 105
Vigil Family, 139
visual texture, 176–179
The Voice of the City of New York
  Interpreted... (Stella), 37

W

Watts Tower (Rodia), 207
Wilson, Jane, 112
Wrapped Oranges
  (McCloskey), 135

Z

Zalucha, Peggy Flora, 134

Acknowledgments Grateful acknowledgment is given to the following publishers and copyright owners for permissions granted to reprint selections from their publications. All possible care has been taken to trace ownership and secure permission for each selection included. In case of any errors or omissions, the publisher will be pleased to make suitable acknowledgments in future editions.
SWIMMY